Weller Pottery

Jeffrey B. Snyder

4880 Lower Valley Road, Atglen, PA 19310 USA

Dedicated to the memories of Donald and Ruby Hall.

Library of Congress Cataloging-in-Publication Data

Snyder, Jeffrey B.
  Weller pottery,: art potter, art ware, ceramic
    p. cm.
  ISBN 0-7643-2186-2 (hardcover)
1. Snyder, catalogs (Firm)—Catalogs. 2. Weller pottery—
Collectors and collecting—Catalogs. I. Title.
NK4210.C365A4 2004
738'.09424'6—dc22
                    20040114107

Designed by Mark David Bowyer
Type set in University Roman Bd BT/Aldine721 BT

ISBN: 0-7643-2186-2
Printed in China
1 2 3 4

Published by Schiffer Publishing Ltd.
4880 Lower Valley Road
Atglen, PA 19310
Phone: (610) 593-1777; Fax: (610) 593-2002
E-mail: Info@schifferbooks.com

For the largest selection of fine reference books on this and
related subjects, please visit our web site at
www.schifferbooks.com
We are always looking for people to write books on new and
related subjects. If you have an idea for a book please
contact us at the above address.

This book may be purchased from the publisher.
Include $3.95 for shipping.
Please try your bookstore first.
You may write for a free catalog.

In Europe, Schiffer books are distributed by
Bushwood Books
6 Marksbury Ave.
Kew Gardens
Surrey TW9 4JF England
Phone: 44 (0) 20 8392-8585; Fax: 44 (0) 20 8392-9876
E-mail: info@bushwoodbooks.co.uk
Free postage in the U.K., Europe; air mail at cost.

Contents

Acknowledgments

Meeting wonderful new people is one of the great joys associated with authorship. While writing and photographing this book, I was supported and assisted by a number of generous, knowledgeable individuals. These people took time from their busy schedules to work with me in amassing the images and details presented in this book. I want to thank them all. Special thanks to: David Rago Auctions and Denise Rago-Wallace; the Cincinnati Art Galleries , LLC and Riley Humler; Ken and Sharon Ballentine; Seekers Antiques; Bob Shores and Dale Jones; Arnie Small and Barbara Gerr; the historians at the Smithsonian Institution; and to those who prefer to remain anonymous.

Special thanks for Doug Congdon-Martin for the photo shoot he conducted on my behalf. Also, I offer my thanks to my editor, Donna Baker, who keeps me on the literary straight and narrow.

I also wish to thank the talented staff at Schiffer Publishing for making this book a work of art. You know who you are! Thanks for everything.

Special thanks to my family, who stand beside me through thick and thin, making it all worthwhile.

Finally, a heartfelt thank you to all you readers out there. Without you ... what would be the point?

Introduction

Spanning over seventy years of production, the pottery firm established as a one-man operation in 1872 in Fultonham, Ohio, by Samuel Augustus Weller, and moved to Zanesville, Ohio, in the following decade, would be lauded as the largest manufacturer of mass-produced artware in the world during the first quarter of the twentieth century. During its lifetime (1872-1948), the S. A. Weller Pottery Company produced art pottery and artwares that changed with the times, reflecting the art movements of the day – these included Arts and Crafts, Art Nouveau, Art Deco, and the beginnings of Modernism. Weller ceramics also reflected the desires and enthusiasms of the middle class public that purchased them. Presented here is a survey of the ceramics produced throughout those many decades.

Among the numerous ware types made were impressive jardinières with pedestals, vases, wall pockets, hanging baskets, umbrella stands, console bowls and candlesticks, novelty items (including figurines of people, cherubs, and animals), lamps, and tobacco jars. Not shy about filling needs where they were found, Weller also produced utilitarian ware and, following the repeal of Prohibition, beer mugs. These wares were decorated in a seemingly endless variety of glazes, hand-painted images, and embossed, molded adornments. Weller ceramics were offered to distributors and the public in "lines," offering a variety of objects of similar form, design, and decorative treatment under a line name, such as "Turada" or "Sicardo." It is said that the inspiration for Weller line names came from many sources, including the names of designers, descriptive names, and even names lifted from passing Pullman cars as trains rumbled through town. The number of items in each line varied. The early art pottery line Louwelsa, produced from 1895 to 1918, was very popular. As the years progressed and demand remained strong, additional items were added until the Louwelsa line included over 500 pieces.

Louwelsa tankard decorated with a portrait of a Native American, identified by a mark at the base as "High Bear Sioux Chief." The art work was painted by Marie Rauchfuss, circa 1905. Other marks include a Louwelsa Weller insignia, the designation "436 7," and the artist's initials painted on the side of the piece. 16.75" h. *Courtesy of Mark Mussio, Cincinnati Art Galleries, LLC.* $1,000-1,500.

Conch shell-shaped wall pocket in turquoise, marked "101". 11.25" x 6". *Courtesy of David Rago Auctions.* $100-200.

Hudson Scenic vase decorated by artist Hester Pillsbury, printed "Weller Pottery" and "half kiln" manufacturer's mark. 15.5" h. *Courtesy of Ken and Sharon Ballentine.* $11,000-13,000.

Hanging basket featuring four finches perched on branches near a stone wall. Unmarked. 4.75" x 9.5". *Courtesy of Mark Mussio, Cincinnati Art Galleries, LLC.* $300-400.

Jap Birdimal umbrella stand in blues and grays. Decorated by tube lining with a scene of trees along a shoreline, all illuminated by a pale yellow moon. Marked "WELLER" in small block letters on the base. *Courtesy of Mark Mussio, Cincinnati Art Galleries, LLC.* $500-700.

Matt Green umbrella stand, unmarked. 20" h. *Courtesy of David Rago Auctions.* $400-600.

Greora console bowl with flower frog. Marked "Weller Pottery" in incised print. c. 1930s. 15" l. *Courtesy of Bob Shores and Dale Jones.* $850.

Three Matt Green pieces: a candlestick with a triangular base; a small vase with tapered neck; and a buttressed planter with impressed detail. The tallest piece measures 8" high. *Courtesy of David Rago Auctions.* $250-350 each.

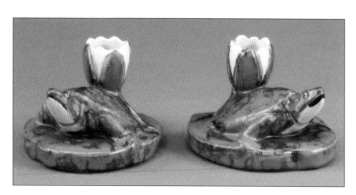

Coppertone turtle and lily pad candlesticks, marked. 3.25" x 5" each. *Courtesy of David Rago Auctions.* $350-500.

Matt Green faceted bottle-shaped lamp base on four feet embossed with two satyr heads, unmarked. 14.5" x 9". *Courtesy of David Rago Auctions.* $650-950.

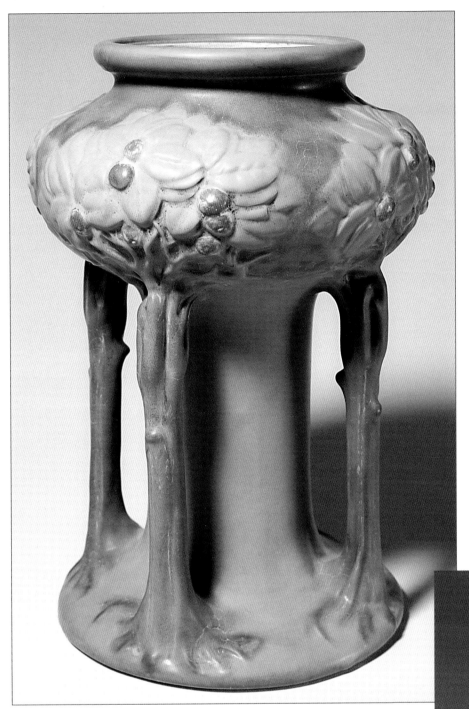

Lamp vase comprised of four fruit laden trees growing from the base to support the bulbous top. Finished in a green mat glaze with black shading and rose colored fruit. Stamped "Weller" in small block letters inside the base. 16.25" h. *Courtesy of Mark Mussio, Cincinnati Art Galleries, LLC.* $1,500-2,000.

Dickens Ware ovoid vase decorated with a woman playing a mandolin on a crescent moon, initialed "J.H." – which could be artist John J. Herold – and identified on the base with a stamped mark. 8.5" h. *Courtesy of David Rago Auctions.* $250-350.

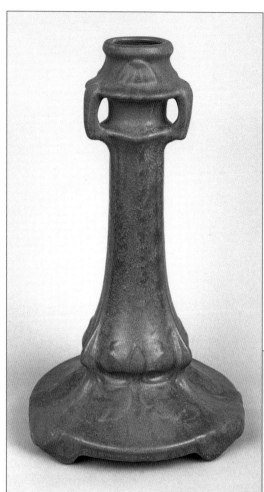

Architectural-style lamp base, Matt Green, unmarked. 13" h. *Courtesy of Arnie Small and Barbara Gerr.* $500+.

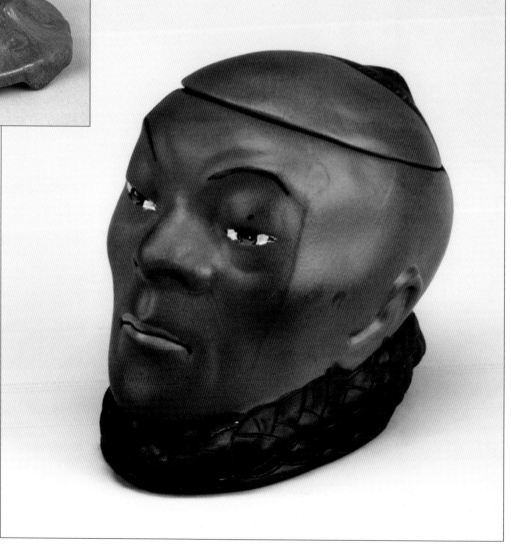

Dickens Ware Chinaman humidor marked "Dickens Weller." 6.25" x 6". *Courtesy of David Rago Auctions.* $1,200-1,500.

The Weller Menagerie

Inspired by the natural world, Weller produced a wide range of figures and figural flower frogs to ornament the house. Here is a sampling of the company's many offerings, ranging from naturalistic to whimsical in their design.

Garden Ware Scottie dog figurine, incised "Weller Pottery" mark. 12" h., 11" paw to tail. *Courtesy of Arnie Small and Barbara Gerr.* $2,500+.

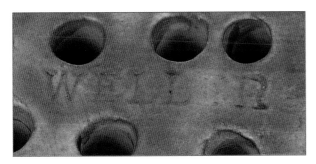

Turtle flower frog, impressed "WELLER" mark. 5.25" long. *Courtesy of Arnie Small and Barbara Gerr.* $330-360.

Turtle flower frog, impressed "WELLER" mark. 10"
l. x 5" h. *Courtesy of Arnie Small and Barbara Gerr.*
$750-825.

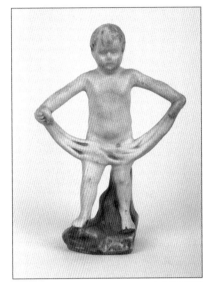

Muskota fisher boy with creel flower frog, hole for rod, unmarked. 6.25" h. *Courtesy of Arnie Small and Barbara Gerr.* $360-480.

Muskota figure of a young nude child with cloth, detailed front and back, unmarked. 5" h. *Courtesy of Arnie Small and Barbara Gerr.* $525-575.

Rare, large "Pop-Eye" dog figure covered in a brown and green feathered matte glaze, unmarked. 4.75" x 11". *Courtesy of David Rago Auctions.* $2,000-3,000.

Flower frog with bird in blue and pink, unmarked. 3.5" h. *Courtesy of David Rago Auctions.* $150-250.

Squirrel on stump bowl, impressed "WELLER" mark. 4.25" h.
Courtesy of Arnie Small and Barbara Gerr. $480-525.

Dragonfly flower frog, unmarked. 4" l. *Courtesy of Arnie Small and Barbara Gerr.* $535-585.

Butterfly flower frog, impressed "WELLER" mark, 4"
d. *Courtesy of Arnie Small and Barbara Gerr.* $535-585.

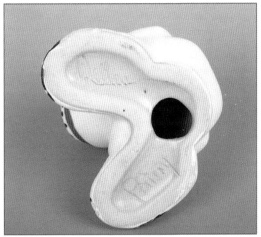

Comic "Pop-eye" figural dog marked in script incised "Weller Pottery." 4.25" h. *Courtesy of Arnie Small and Barbara Gerr.* $480-525.

Cats on fence with flowerpots, impressed "WELLER" mark, 7" h.
Courtesy of Arnie Small and Barbara Gerr. $990-1,090.

Swan and kingfisher flower frogs, impressed "WELLER" marks. Kingfisher: 6.5" h. *Courtesy of Arnie Small and Barbara Gerr.* $390-430 each.

Kingfisher flower frog, printed
"Weller" semi-circular "half kiln" mark
with "1" on base. 9" h. *Courtesy of Arnie
Small and Barbara Gerr.* $390-430.

White flower frog, two geese with spread wings, printed circular "full kiln" mark reading "Weller Ware." 7" l., 4.5" h. *Courtesy of Arnie Small and Barbara Gerr.* $660-725.

Unusual goose figural with head turned back. (All Weller figures have glazed ceramic eyes.) 12" h. *Courtesy of Arnie Small and Barbara Gerr.* NP (**N**o **P**rice).

Two piece dog and stand figural marked with an impressed "WELLER" on each piece. 6.5" h. together and 6" across the base. *Courtesy of Arnie Small and Barbara Gerr.* $550+.

Robin flower frog, impressed "WELLER" mark. 6.5" l. x 5" h. *Courtesy of Arnie Small and Barbara Gerr.* $420-460.

Muskota water fowl on log fish bowl
holder with glass fish bowl, impressed
"WELLER" mark, 11" h. x 8.5" long.
This glass bowl is an after market
insert designed for this piece. *Courtesy
of Arnie Small and Barbara Gerr.* $800+.

Samuel A. Weller sought out and employed some very talented individuals, a number who would go on to make bigger names for themselves elsewhere in later years. Among the luminaries were Henry Schmidt, who developed the Turada line, the first ware decorated using a squeeze bag slip trail technique in the Ohio valley; Charles Upjohn, who developed two Dickens Ware lines at the turn of the twentieth century; Jacques Sicard, a French glaze expert who had produced metallic luster glazes for Clement Massier during the majolica craze and who created the lustrous Sicardo line for Weller that made a big impression on attendees of the 1904 Louisiana Purchase Exposition in St. Louis; Frederick Hürton Rhead, an English artist who developed the Jap Birdimal line for Weller and would go on the create Fiesta in later years for Homer Laughlin in West Virginia; Rudolph Lorber, creator of naturalistic lines including Muskota, Forest, and Glendale; Dorothy England Laughead, creator of Chase, Silvertone, and Garden Animals lines; and John Lessell, who as head of the decorating department developed luster glaze lines such as LaSa, Cloudburst, and Lamar.

Turada oil lamp shaped vessel. 6" x 9.5". *Courtesy of David Rago Auctions.* $250-350.

Dickens Ware pillow vase, possibly by Charles Upjohn, incised and painted with a mallard on the shore, impressed manufacturer's mark and several artist's marks. 5" x 5.5". *Courtesy of David Rago Auctions.* $400-600.

Opposite page and above:
Dickens Ware, Second Line, vase by Charles Upjohn, featuring an inscription for Sir Fredric Landseer, with a "C.B. Upjohn" signature, and marked with an impressed "Dickens Ware Weller" mark. 13.5" h. *Courtesy of Ken and Sharon Ballentine.* $2,600-2,900.

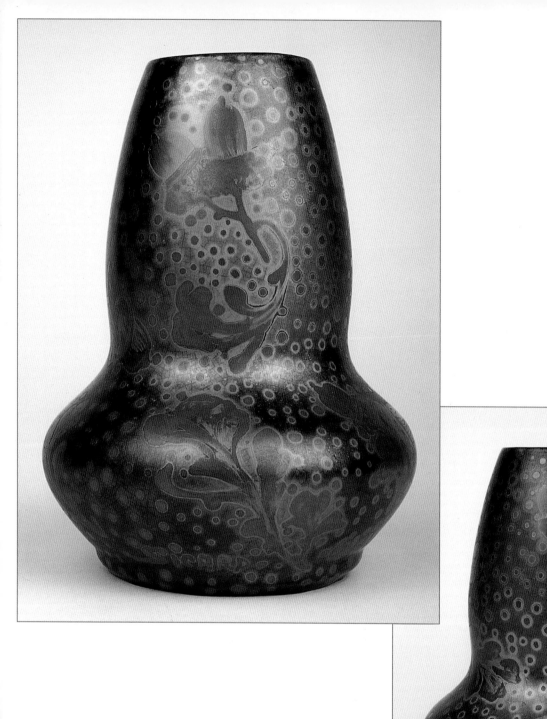

Sicardo vase, signed by the artist
on the side at the base, "Sicard."
6.5" h. *Courtesy of Seekers Antiques.*
$1,850-2,035.

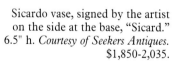

Muskota flower frog featuring a frog in a flower, unmarked. 4.75" h. *Courtesy of Arnie Small and Barbara Gerr.* $420-460.

Jap Birdimal three-handled bulbous vase decorated in squeeze bag technique with stylized green, brown, and white trees on a teal blue ground, identified with an incised "Weller Faience E500 1/2" and an artist's "OMN" marks. 8.25" x 5.5". *Courtesy of David Rago Auctions.* $1,000-1,500.

Three Forest jardinières, unmarked. Largest, 8.25" d. *Courtesy of Arnie Small and Barbara Gerr.* Back: $300-330; left: $250-275; right: $210-230.

Rare Silvertone jardinière decorated with hydrangea, identified with a full-kiln stamped mark. 11" x 10.5". *Courtesy of David Rago Auctions.* $750-1,000.

Unusual LaSa tall vase painted with bamboo and waves, marked "Weller LaSa." 12.5" x 6". *Courtesy of David Rago Auctions.* $600-900.

John Lessell's Lusterware scenic vase, probably made at the Weller Pottery, showing leafy trees against a lake and mountain backdrop. Signed at base by the artist but otherwise unmarked. 10.25". *Courtesy of Mark Mussio, Cincinnati Art Galleries, LLC.* $200-300.

What Is Art Pottery and Artware?

Already in the introduction, the terms art pottery and artware have been bandied about. Art pottery in America originated in Ohio in the 1870s, taking inspiration from the Arts and Crafts Movement's desire to create handcrafted beauty to counter the increasingly mechanized lifestyle of an industrialized age. Well-educated Victorian women took up pottery decoration with enthusiasm to fill their free time, helping to push the early development of art pottery forward. Art pottery is decorative ware that has the appearance of being handmade (the degree to which it was made by hand varied from one pottery firm to another) and features hand decoration including images from nature, soft glaze color transitions, and a Japanese design sensibility. (Japanese influence on American design stemmed from the 1876 Philadelphia Centennial Exhibition where Japanese wares were first displayed to large audiences in the United States.)

Louwelsa vase finely painted by L. Blake with a Saint Bernard, stamped "LOUWELSA WELLER," signed "L. Blake." 10.5" x 6". *Courtesy of David Rago Auctions.* $600-900.

Artware developed over time from art pottery. Artware ceramics are mass-produced, using molds to form the bodies; they are decorated with striking glazes and limited hand decoration. Artware develops out of the potter's need to reduce production costs, increase output to meet demand, and expand the clientele by producing decorative wares at lower costs available to a broader range of consumers. The mass production techniques employed reduced the overall number of skilled artists required to make a given piece of pottery, thereby both lowering the cost and reducing production time.

Also at work as time passed and economic and social conditions changed was a demand for ceramics more compatible with a simplified lifestyle. The ideals of handcrafted workmanship espoused by art movements and embodied in art pottery were replaced by necessity with the more economical, mass-produced artwares the public sought to accompany their changing lifestyle.

Atlas flaring star-shaped bowl in blue and ivory, marked. 6" x 9.25". *Courtesy of David Rago Auctions.* $150-250.

In the trade journal *Ceramic Industry*, Glen Lukens spoke to the difference between art pottery and artware very bluntly from his perspective in August 1945. Of art pottery, he said,

> …art potters discouraged distribution in prewar days by the outrageous prices they asked. They had the notion that they possessed a little more of the divine essence than other people and held inflexible ideas about altering their designs an iota, even though the change would help sales. They were geared only to limited production, not too reliably on schedule. And they were unable to comprehend the pressure for volume that made the production of the small pottery of puny consequence to harassed sales representatives and buyers.

Two-handled bulbous vase with flowers, marked with a half-kiln stamp. 8" x 6.75". *Courtesy of David Rago Auctions.* $200-300.

Speaking in favor of artware manufacturing techniques, Lukens admonished,

Remembering that he [the potter] is a business-man, as well as an artist and technician, he must study production costs against the day when prices will have to be shaved to meet competition. He needs smoother, steadier, more controllable methods of production as a means to surer output and alleviating delivery disappointments. From organization and recognition, he must seek professional stimulation. And, finally, he must study the market so as to be able to understand buyers' problems and work with them on common ground.

Bulbous vase embossed with leaves under a deep rose matte glaze, identified with a stamped mark. 6" x 4.75". *Courtesy of David Rago Auctions.* $600-800.

When studying Weller ceramics, one may observe the gradual transition from art pottery production of the late nineteenth through the early twentieth century to ever-increasing use of the mass production techniques of artware, including an increase in molded relief decoration beginning in 1905 and the elimination of free-hand decoration by the early 1930s. Samuel A. Weller's company produced a great deal of decorative ceramics – pottery fully intended to be priced within the reach of the vast majority of middle class consumers. In doing so, Weller followed a fundamental principle of the Arts and Crafts Movement, to create art that was affordable to all.

Influential Art Movements

In 1872, when Samuel Weller established his one-man operation, he produced the utilitarian wares many potters started with. These were useful jugs and pots sold to neighbors in rural and urban settings. However, following the expansion of Weller's operation and move to Zanesville, Ohio, by the 1890s Weller's company was producing art pottery, following the lead of both Rookwood Pottery and the work of William A. Long. Weller was creating pottery in copious amounts in the mid-1890s, producing an eye-catching iridescent glaze combining different metallic lusters. The Arts and Crafts Movement heavily influenced this early pottery.

The Arts and Crafts Movement was a reaction to industrialization. As the Industrial Revolution swept through Western society, families attracted by new job opportunities moved from rural to urban communities, radically changing their daily lives and routines. Husbands and wives who had once worked side by side on the land were separated, he going off to work in the factory or office and she left to tend to the home or to take up job opportunities that were slowly opening to women. Families were distanced from the land. Many, living in crowded, dirty cities and working in poor conditions for low wages, looked back wistfully to an earlier, simpler, agrarian age. Industrialization brought with it a wide range of low quality, mass-produced wares as well. Those seeking to explain the low product quality observed that without any single person following a product from beginning to end in the modern factory, no individual took pride in the end result. Without concern for the finished product, the results were shoddy.

The Arts and Crafts Movement originated in England by the 1880s and spread to the United States, inspired by the teachings and examples of William Morris and John Ruskin. The ideal of the movement was to allow individual artists the opportunity to create wares in the decorative arts that were beautifully handcrafted products from nature. Such products were to be both useful objects and works of art. The decorative motifs taken from nature reflect that desire for closeness with the natural world that was largely lost in the urban setting. As members of a social movement, Arts and Crafts practitioners sought to improve working conditions, free artists to be creative, and bring affordable quality art to all peoples. It was also hoped that the presence of art would elevate social values.

The Arts and Crafts Movement would remain influential in the United States into the first quarter of the twentieth century. Weller was one of the potteries that picked up on the Arts and Crafts philosophy, producing art pottery in lower price ranges accessible to many in the middle class.

Rare Matt Green jardinière embossed with four handles styled as Arts & Crafts strap handles, unmarked. 9.75" x 12". *Courtesy of David Rago Auctions.* $300-400.

Eocean wine carafe (lid missing) decorated by Frank Ferrell with lush purple grapes; marked "Weller 9002" on the base and signed by the artist on the side. 11.5". *Courtesy of Mark Mussio, Cincinnati Art Galleries, LLC.* $800-1,000.

While the Arts and Crafts Movement rebelled against the industrialization and lowering of social values in Victorian Society, Art Nouveau (1890-1914) railed against the Victorian penchant for designing objects steeped in the antiquarian's historicism (pulling designs and motifs from the ancients and applying them to new wares) – a common trend in early majolica ceramics introduced in the 1850s and popular through the 1880s, first in England and later in the United States. Gardens, both the large public and small private varieties, were extremely popular in the Victorian age. Nature, well tamed and neatly kept, was viewed with a romantic eye. Art Nouveau designers took to the gardens and the natural world beyond for their inspiration. The results were decorative wares taking their forms from nature rather than history. Straight-lined precision symmetry was replaced with asymmetrical, sinuous, botanical … and even faunal … forms. Divorced from the designs of the past, Art Nouveau was considered truly modern. Weller pottery displays attributes of Art Nouveau during this period.

The Art Nouveau Movement also recognized the stressful nature of the urban lifestyle. It was believed that interior rooms decorated in the Art Nouveau style would offer a restful interior space, providing the peace of nature (with none of its pitfalls) to all who resided there. Therefore, the home or public space adorned in Art Nouveau style would be therapeutic to the frazzled nerves of modern humanity.

Art Deco was the style most influential between 1925 and the beginning of World War II. Geometric forms and lavish decorative techniques were the early hallmarks of Art Deco. It was at the Paris Exposition of 1925 (the Exposition des Arts Décoratifs et Industriels Modernes) that the public was made aware of Art Deco. Exhibitions of this sort had long been used both to show the public the best of modern design and to give international competitors a chance to compare products and glean new trends. It became clear in Paris that the organic Art Nouveau lines were being replaced with the geometric, streamlined forms and rich decoration of Art Deco.

Lorbeek four piece console set consisting of a 3" x 13.75" bowl, a 5" flower holder, and two 2.5" candle holders, all in an Art Deco style of stepped geometric form and covered with a lavender semi-gloss glaze. Marked with a "Weller Ware" blue ink stamp manufacturer's mark. *Courtesy of Mark Mussio, Cincinnati Art Galleries, LLC.* $200-300.

Art Deco style would reach its height of popularity and influence in 1935. In America, the Depression brought Art Deco styling to new forms. Many Americans found themselves cash-strapped and in no mood to purchase expensive luxuries in a lavish, new streamlined style. As a result, Art Deco motifs were incorporated into simple, durable, mass-produced, and vividly glazed ceramics that could be purchased for a song. Frederick Hürten Rhead's description of his interpretation of Art Deco ware sums up the American Art Deco style well, "… an easy going informal series of articles, smart enough to fit in any house and obvious enough to furnish spots of emphasis …" (Rhead 1937)

The simplified, streamlined forms of Art Deco reflected the streamlining of society as well. The Victorians' fondness for elaborate social strictures and formal behavior was abandoned in favor of a more relaxed lifestyle requiring fewer accoutrements. In part, this was society bowing to necessity, as the Depression era of the 1930s limited middle class consumers' buying power and made the formal dinner parties thrown by their Victorian grandparents an impossibility. Replacing such fancy dinners and the imposing, costly Victorian homes complete with servants (at least one "maid of all works" and a cook) were bungalows, outdoor barbeques, and help-yourself buffets.

By the late 1930s, Art Deco was being replaced by a style that has come to be known as "mid-century modern." The forms were considered organic, free-form, and futuristic. They used the plasticity of clay to great advantage, creating soft, rounded shapes and curling rims. The lines were smooth and decoration was kept to a minimum. The movement was seen as an attempt to create a truly American style, one completely devoid of elements derived from overseas. Competition from foreign potters was on the rise, with low cost ceramics arriving in ever-greater numbers on American shores. This movement attempted to stem the tide, providing home-grown, imaginative, distinctive wares to tempt American consumers away from cheap foreign pottery. Russel Wright endeavored to set the stage for the new movement with his American Way show, which opened in 1940 and closed roughly one year later. The American Way exhibition featured the best modern American designs in the decorative arts.

Of Bodies, Glazes, and Marks

Weller ceramics were produced with earthenware bodies. Earthenware is soft, fired in kilns at relatively low temperatures, and water absorbent. Glazes consisting of lead sulfides with additives introduced to add color or opacity to an otherwise colorless and transparent medium were applied over earthenware bodies to render them impermeable to water and more resistant to chipping.

Glaze coloring throughout much of potting history was more art than science. The Chinese and Egyptians were known for their early work in glaze colors. Iron compounds, creating reds and browns, have long been among the main coloring agents. Until the eighteenth century, the only other metals that could produce red glazes were gold and copper. The Chinese were early users of copper oxides to create their distinctive deep red glazes. Many art potteries strove to recreate these Chinese red glazes. John Lessell, art director at Weller from 1920-1924, has been credited with creating Weller's version of Chinese red glazing with his Chengtu line.

Both the Chinese and Persians were using cobalt by the ninth century A.D. to create a deep, brilliant blue. For centuries, cobalt was the only color that would withstand the high heat of firing when used as underglaze decoration. The French would begin using cobalt in the fifteenth century and England's Staffordshire potters would use cobalt to great effect from 1750 onward.

Additionally, copper was used to create turquoise, green, and blue; antimony for yellow; chromium came into use after 1802 for a dark green and was mixed with other metals to create pinks and crimsons; gold was used to create pink, maroon, and purple from the seventeenth century onward. Despite all this glaze color creation over the centuries, scientific methods were not applied to glaze formulation until the nineteenth century.

Rare Matt Green corseted vase with reticulated and embossed poppy decoration, unmarked. 12.25" x 6.5". *Courtesy of David Rago Auctions.* $950-1,250.

Unusual vase covered in matte green glaze over a Silvertone blank, unmarked. 7" x 6". *Courtesy of David Rago Auctions.* $500-600.

Matt Green planter of architectural form with ribbed bands to body and buttressed handles, unmarked. 7" x 10". *Courtesy of David Rago Auctions.* $450-650.

The formulas for successful, popular glaze colors that were not prohibitively expensive to reproduce and that were relatively reliable in their end results were jealously guarded at Weller and the other art potteries of the late nineteenth and twentieth centuries. Experimentation was constant, as the many Weller glazes attest to. Consistency of color was a challenge as it was influenced by many factors, ranging from consistent measurements of coloring agents to proper, steady heat in the kilns. The many variations in Weller glazes prove the point.

Another trait common to art potteries was the marking of the bases or undersides of their products with manufacturer's marks. Such marks identified the company that produced the ware and, at times, included the line name of the products marked. Manufacturer's marks are convenient for identification and were changed over time if a company survived for a considerable period. These changes in manufacturer's marks help collectors to identify the wares of different periods of production. Weller wares have been divided into three periods: early (1895-1918); middle (1918-1935); and late (1935-1948). In this way, Weller ceramics may be organized into periods and the changes in style over time may be observed more clearly.

Manufacturer's marks were useful to the company as they identified their product for consumers. As America became an increasingly mobile society, people relocating across the country sought out the familiar wherever they went. It was reassuring to find familiar names in strange places. Once consumers associated a particular manufacturer's name or product's name with quality and reliability, they tended to stick with that name brand. It behooved Weller to mark their wares.

However, not all pieces bear manufacturer's marks. Some items were simply too small to be marked. If items were sold in sets, there was no need to mark every piece in that set. And, on occasion, companies produced certain inexpensive items that helped pay the bills but that the firm would rather not be associated with publicly.

Accompanying Weller's manufacturer's marks at times on hand decorated wares are artist's signatures or monograms. Dr. Edwin Atlee Barber (1851-1916), ceramics scholar, curator, and director of the Pennsylvania Museum of Art, recorded many manufacturer's marks and artist's monograms in his book *Marks of American Potters*. Dr. Barber was considered so influential in the potting community that to be recorded in one of his several books was considered a coup.

Values

The prices found in the captions are in United States dollars. Prices vary immensely based on the location of the market, the venue of the sale, the rarity of the items and/or their glaze treatments, and the enthusiasms of the collecting community. Prices in the Midwest differ from those in the West or East, and those at specialty shows or auctions will differ from those in dealer's shops or through dealer's web pages.

All of these factors make it impossible to create absolutely accurate prices listings, but a guide to realistic pricing may be offered. Please note: these values are not provided to set prices in the antiques marketplace, but rather to give the reader a reasonable idea of what one might expect to pay for mint condition Weller pottery.

That being said, here are a few Weller rarities to pique the interest. In 2003, a Louwelsa umbrella stand decorated in grapes on the vine, measuring 23" high, and signed by Frank Ferrell, the artist who decorated it, held an estimated value of $1,600-1,800. A rare Weller skull-shaped humidor was appraised in 2000 at $2,000-3,000. A Hudson scenic vase, measuring 8-5/8" high, hand decorated by Hester Pillsbury with a Spanish sailing ship and two other vessels, sold at auction in 1997 for $4,510. A Weller pelican garden ornament sold in 2002 at auction for $16,100. However, beating them all was a monumental Weller Aurelian vase, measuring 6' 8-1/2" high, hand decorated with apples on the branch by Frank Ferrell (who signed and dated it), and used as an exhibition piece for the 1904 Louisiana Purchase Exposition (where it won the Gold Medal in the arts category), sold at auction in 1997 for $112,500. Happy hunting!

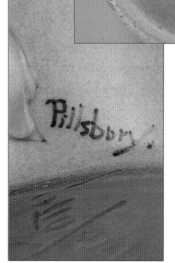

Hudson vase decorated by Hester Pillsbury and signed "Pillsbury" near the base. The bumblebee on the back is an unusual addition to the floral motif, incised "Weller Pottery" script mark on the base. 12" h. *Courtesy of Ken and Sharon Ballentine.* $3,400-3,700.

Weller Ware and Usage

Here both the company's history and the wares produced over decades of potting are revealed together. The discussion of product lines touches on the company's highlights and does not try to be all-inclusive. The chapter is organized into subheadings by the three recognized periods of Weller production, which show Weller's transition from art pottery to artware. The early period is shown beginning in 1895 as this begins Weller's serious foray into art pottery.

Ohio Art Pottery

In the late nineteenth century, eastern Ohio had what it took to become a thriving center of pottery production. Natural deposits of clay, coal, and gas were abundant and transportation by river and rail was readily accessible. Zanesville, Ohio, was particularly well situated for the pottery business. The natural resources were present, the city was located along the Muskingum River, at the mouth of the Licking River, and was served by the following railroads: the Baltimore and Ohio; Pennsylvania; Cleveland, Akron & Columbus; Ohio River & Western; Wheeling & Lake Erie; Zanesville & Western; and Ohio & Little Kanawha. A series of locks and dams on the Muskingum River allowed small ships access to both the Ohio River and the Ohio Canal. Shipping ceramics to market was not a problem. So many potteries found Zanesville the ideal home that the city was nicknamed "Clay City."

Given these conditions and the number of potteries working in Ohio, it should be no surprise that Ohio was the center of the art pottery movement in the United States. Ohio State University founded the first school for ceramics in 1894. The first of the art potteries was established in Cincinnati, Ohio, by Maria Longworth Nichols in 1880. Nichols intended Rookwood to produce handmade art from the potting wheel. Profit was considered secondary to the artistry of the pottery produced. Nichols and her artists experimented with underglaze decorations. As a real accomplishment, at the Paris World's Fair of 1889, Rookwood Pottery took a gold medal for their work.

Generally speaking, early art pottery tended to be signed by the artist who decorated it, or was given that artist's monogram. However, as time passed and art pottery slipped into the more technically produced artware, artist's signatures and monograms disappeared. While it took an artist to hand decorate early art pottery, a trained worker applied the glazes and simpler decorative treatments of artware in anonymity.

Bird's-eye view of Zanesville, Ohio, the "Clay City," taken on April 3, 1913. *Courtesy of Library of Congress, Prints and Photographs Division* [DLC/PP-1913:44590].

Weller's Early Period, 1895-1918

Beginning Years—1872-1890

Born in 1851 into a farming family, Samuel A. Weller established his fledgling pottery operation in Fultonham, Ohio, in 1872. Weller himself originally handled all aspects of production, from the initial excavation of the clays to the final delivery of the finished product to market. As with most upstart Midwestern pottery operations of this period, Weller's first products were strictly utilitarian, including flowerpots, jars, jugs, tiles, and other wares useful on the farm and in town. As his business grew, Samuel Weller moved his operations to Zanesville, "Clay City," Ohio, during the 1880s. By 1890 he had a three-story facility on Putnam Commons in Zanesville, employing sixty persons to handle the growing business.

Of Artists and Their Wares, 1895-1918

Inspired by the close association with many other local pottery firms, the early Weller product lines expanded in style and form to include hanging baskets, umbrella stands, and more. By the mid-1890s, the company would make its first foray into art pottery. The inspiration for this move came at the 1893 Columbian Exposition in Chicago, Illinois. Manufacturers attended world's fairs in part to gain ideas and techniques from their competitors. At the Exposition, Samuel Weller was impressed by the display of "Lonhuda" art pottery, produced by William A. Long's Lonhuda Pottery in Stubenville, Ohio. Moving quickly, the two men came to an agreement. Lonhuda art pottery was to be produced at the S. A. Weller Pottery Company factory and William Long would design for Samuel Weller. However, the association with Long dissolved in 1896. With the birth of Samuel Weller's daughter Louise that very year, the art pottery produced in the form and with the decoration of Lonhuda was renamed Louwelsa after Long's departure. As art pottery enthusiasts know, the name Louwelsa was a fusion of several names, combining the first three letters of Louise, the first three of Weller, and Samuel A. Weller's first and middle initials. Louwelsa combined high gloss glaze colors in browns and yellows, making clever use of highlights and shading. Over the deep background glazes were deftly painted images from nature and striking portraits, using vivid green, blue, and red glazes. Among the most desirable Louwelsa wares today are those adorned with portraiture or images of game animals, fish, and birds. So popular was Louwelsa from its introduction that it would remain a thriving company line from 1895 to 1918. Over the course of production, over 500 items would be offered in the Louwelsa line. That is a great deal of art pottery.

Lonhuda ruffled rim bowl decorated with hand-painted yellow blossoms found on both the exterior and interior of the bowl, identified with a stamped "Lonhuda/LF" mark. 2.5" x 7". *Courtesy of David Rago Auctions.* $165-275.

Louwelsa mug painted with a portrait of an Arabian man, with a stamped mark. 6.5" x 4.5". *Courtesy of David Rago Auctions.* $300-500.

Louwelsa vase decorated with vining Nasturtiums, painted by Anna Fulton Best, impressed with the circular "Weller Louwelsa" circular seal and raised numbers "579" on the base, while the artist's initials are painted on the side of the vase. 14". *Courtesy of Mark Mussio, Cincinnati Art Galleries, LLC.* $300-400.

In 1895, Charles Babcock Upjohn hired on as Weller's art director. He would remain with the firm until 1905, later turning to professorial pursuits at Columbia University. During his tenure at Weller, Charles Upjohn produced the popular Dickens Ware lines. As English potters had been inspired to produce ceramics based on porcelains imported from China to England centuries before, Samuel Weller took inspiration from a line of ceramics the English pottery firm Doulton was producing in the late 1800s and exporting to America. The line included tableware, accessories, and figurines decorated with characters from Charles Dickens's tales. Samuel Weller turned to Charles Upjohn to create ceramics decorated with Dickensian characters as well. Before the end of its run, there would be three Dickens Ware lines; the first two were Upjohn's creations, while the third was said to be produced under the guidance of the English immigrant potter, Frederick Hürten Rhead. The first Dickens Ware line was produced on shapes similar to the Louwelsa offerings, glazed in solid background colors of brown, blue, or green, and adorned with underglazed slip painted decorations. These pieces were marked Dickens Ware and were manufactured from 1897 to 1898.

The second Dickens Ware line followed quickly and was continued until 1905. Produced by Upjohn, this line featured incised, sgraffito-type decoration that was applied by hand using sharp tools. The patterns were transferred from paper templates and were again based on the illustrations from Charles Dickens's tales. The underglaze decoration was slip-painted in natural colors over a background of blended colors including a deep brown blending into blue-green or turquoise, or any of these colors alone. There was quite a range of additional colors used, many quite rarely found. The decoration was covered in glaze finishes ranging from soft matt and semi-gloss to a less frequently encountered high gloss.

Tall Dickens Ware cylindrical vase painted with tulips on swirling stems, stamped "570." 14.5" x 4". *Courtesy of David Rago Auctions.* $1,350-1,750.

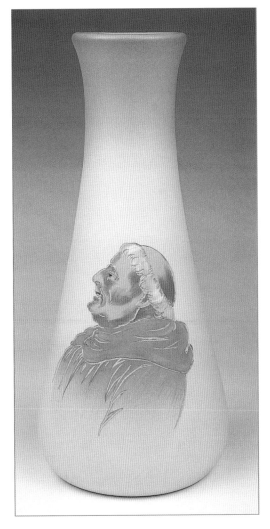

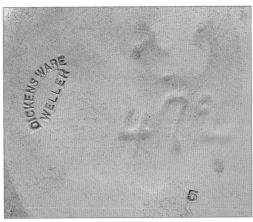

Dickens Ware, Second Line, vase with unusual coloration and no artist's signature. Perhaps this is a crossover piece. It is identified with an impressed "Dickens Ware Weller" mark. 13" h. *Courtesy of Ken and Sharon Ballentine.* $1,700-2,000.

The Eocean line was introduced in 1898. Similar to Louwelsa, it featured blended background colors in different hues, grays, greens, or blues, applied with an atomizer. Hand decorations of figures, flowers, and fruit were added beneath the glaze to complete the look.

The third Dickens Ware line was introduced c. 1904 using the Eocean color palette. Attributed to Rhead in his brief tenure as head designer at Weller (1903-1904), this third line also featured underglaze decorations of Dickensian characters hand painted and sealed beneath a high gloss glaze. A raised disk was placed on the back of each piece featuring the name of the character and the tale from which that character was derived. At times two disks were applied, the second disk bearing a cameo of Charles Dickens himself.

Eocean vase with mauve and mauve & white pansies painted by William Stemm, whose initials are found on the side. Incised "Eocean Weller" mark on the base. 9" h. *Courtesy of Mark Mussio, Cincinnati Art Galleries, LLC.* $300-400.

Dickens Ware, Third Line, bell-shaped vase painted with a figure of man, and two medallions on the back, one a cameo of Charles Dickens, the other marked "Mr. Weller Sr. Pickwick Papers." The vase is identified with a "60-15 WELLER" mark. 8" x 7.25". *Courtesy of David Rago Auctions.* $750-950.

Not every subject to decorate Dickens Ware was a literary character. Some were anonymous tavern dwellers, Native Americans, monks, golfers, and an assortment of wildlife ranging from fish to fowl. Karl Kappes was responsible for some of these designs after Charles Upjohn's departure.

Right and opposite page:
Dickens Ware, Second Line, vase decorated with a Native American and an inscription reading: "Diego Narango, Santa Clara Pueblo," impressed mark "Dickens Ware Weller." 11" h. *Courtesy of Ken and Sharon Ballentine.* $3,000-3,300.

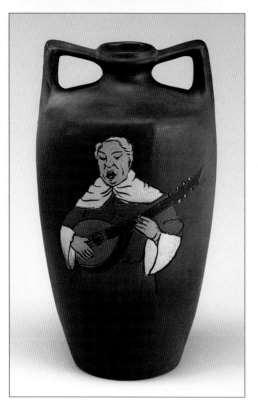

Dickens Ware two-handled vase incised with a monk playing the mandolin, impressed "Dickens Ware Weller" mark. 10" x 5". *Courtesy of David Rago Auctions.* $500-750.

In the early twentieth century, Samuel Weller brought Jacques Sicard and his assistant Henri Gellie from France, where they had worked for Clement Massier on an iridescent, metallic lustrous glaze for Massier's Reflets Metalliques. Weller sought a version of this eye-catching glaze for himself. Arriving in Ohio in 1902, the duo set about their work behind locked doors, creating the metallic lusterware line dubbed Sicardo. Sicardo decoration was Art Nouveau in style, consisting of geometric designs and floral patterns within the glaze. Striking glaze colors included iridescent blue, bronze, crimson, flame, green, purple, and rose. These lustrous glazes adorned bonbon dishes, bowls, candlesticks, jardinières, jewel boxes, plaques, umbrella stands, and vases. Every item was sure to add a grace note to the room it occupied.

Sicardo was first offered in the fall of 1903 and would remain on the market until 1917. Difficult and expensive to produce, this line was sold through jewelry stores, including Tiffany's. Sicardo items were marked with either Sicard or Sicardo for identification and with the Weller company name. Additionally, special order items were signed J. Sicard. This signature was either worked into the design or incised into the design once it was in place. In 1907, Jacques Sicard returned to France. Henri Gellie and his family followed at a later time.

Dickens Ware three-sided vase incised with a swimming fish, identified with a stamped mark. 7" x 4.75". *Courtesy of David Rago Auctions.* $350-450.

THE S. A. WELLER CO.
POTTERY
SALES DEPARTMENT

17941

Zanesville, O., _____ 193___

Name_____

Sold by_____

Quan.	ARTICLE	AMOUNT

THE SHELBY SALESBOOK CO., SHELBY, OHIO —85768△

Sicardo sold through jewelry stores. Weller Pottery Company Sales Department receipt book. 7" x 4". *Courtesy of Mark Mussio, Cincinnati Art Galleries, LLC.* $100-150.

Rare and exceptional Sicard vase with "blown-out" nasturtiums under a metallic finish. Signed "Weller Sicard" on the side. 11" h. *Courtesy of Mark Mussio, Cincinnati Art Galleries, LLC.* $4,000-5,000.

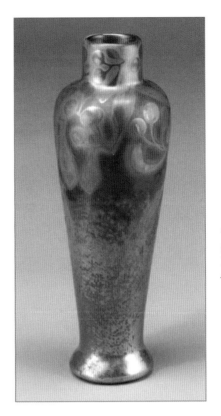

Tall Sicard vase with mistletoe, marked "Weller Sicard" in script. 10" x 3". *Courtesy of David Rago Auctions.* $750-1,000.

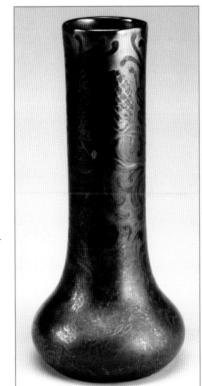

Rare Sicard bottle-shaped vase with pine bows in a luster green, red, and gold, signed Weller. 13.75" x 6.25". *Courtesy of David Rago Auctions.* $1,600-1,900.

Frederick Hürten Rhead was born on August 29, 1880, into a potting family living in Hanley, Stoke-on-Trent, England. Several family members were art directors and designers for large English pottery works. Frederick Rhead's early years were spent apprenticing under his father's supervision at Brownfields Pottery in Burslem. In 1899, Frederick Rhead rose to art director at Wardle & Company while assisting his father in the establishment of a studio for Wileman & Company in Longton. In 1902, Frederick Rhead would travel to the United States for a long and illustrious career. He began working with American art potteries – 1903 and 1904 at Weller, then on to Roseville. Following that, Rhead would teach at the People's University at St. Louis, move on to California to work with Arequipa Pottery and American Encaustic Tiling Company, prior to his last move, to Newell, West Virginia, and the Homer Laughlin China Company.

During his stay at Weller, aside from his association with the third Dickens Ware line, Rhead used a tube lining technique to create the Jap Birdimal and Weller Rhead Faience lines. Rhead's work was inscribed with his last name in blue slip while the Weller name was impressed into the clay.

Jap Birdimal jardinière with cobalt trees under a full moon against a light blue ground, stamped "WELLER" mark. 11.5" x 13.5". *Courtesy of David Rago Auctions.* $450-650.

Rhead Faience vase with incised and painted geese and stylized flowers, incised "Weller Faience" and "Rhead" marks on the base. 8.75" h. *Courtesy of Mark Mussio, Cincinnati Art Galleries, LLC.* $1,500-2,000.

Jap Birdimal pedestal with cobalt trees against a light blue and pink ground. 16.5". *Courtesy of David Rago Auctions.* $450-650.

Weller provided a display for the 1904 Louisiana Purchase Exposition in St. Louis. Knowing how large a draw these world's fairs were, Samuel Weller guaranteed he would hold viewers fascinated by displaying a complete pottery operation in progress. For the judges, Weller displayed the aforementioned 6' 8-1/2" high Aurelian vase decorated by Frank Ferrell. The vase made the proper impression and won the company a gold medal. Such awards added to a company's prestige and were considered significant enough that many firms created a permanent touring stock of high quality products to take from fair to fair over the years.

This panoramic view of the 1904 Louisiana Purchase Exposition at St. Louis was photographed from the roof of the Exposition's Festival Hall. This image first appeared in *Collier's Weekly* on April 24, 1904. *Courtesy of the Library of Congress, Prints and Photographs Division* [LC-USZ62-52827 DLC (left section); -52828 (left center section); -52829 (right center section); -52830 (right section)].

Art Pottery and the Smithsonian Institution

Once the art potteries had their touring stocks in place to display at world's, national, and regional fairs, they turned to museums as another avenue through which their prestige might be enhanced and the public might be exposed to their wares in significant numbers. Many art potteries between 1880 and 1913 donated examples of their work to the Smithsonian's permanent collection.

As might be expected, the first art pottery to enter the Smithsonian's collection came from the Rookwood Pottery Company, dating from 1885. A Weller vase entered the collection in 1906. Weller representative E. A. Jones insisted that the vase contributed by his firm "...should be treated as to advertise the S. A. Weller Pottery." (Lilienfeld 2001, 2-3, par. 6) Each pottery donating items had high hopes their exhibited ware would impress the public and encourage consumers to purchase their products. Considering the Smithsonian's National Museum drew an audience of 225,000 in 1900, this seems to have been a reasonable expectation.

Upon inquiry, the curator of ceramics at the Smithsonian's National Museum of American History, Behring Center, reported that a paper label on the base of the donated vase reads "Russett Matt 10," identifying the glaze color. While the Weller vase was not on display at the museum at the time of this writing, a photograph of this piece appeared in the Spring/May 2001 (Vol. 14, No. 2) issue of *Style 1900* magazine on page 41. (Curator of ceramics 2004)

That vase was not the only example of Weller production to end up in the Smithsonian's collection. Jacques Sicard asked a friend in Ohio to donate one of his St. Cecelia metallic lusterware wall plaques, produced by Weller, to a "...typical American Institution." (Lilienfeld 2001, 3, par. 2) The Smithsonian Institution was his friend's choice to meet the criteria.

In 1905, when the company was six hundred employees strong and offering twenty-two product lines, the decision was made to reduce reliance on hand painted decorations in favor of relief molded decoration. The era of Upjohn, Sicard, and Rhead was largely over. From this point forward, greater volume was produced at lower cost by keeping the decoration simple enough that semi-skilled laborers could successfully apply it. Without the need for skilled artists as decorators, the company was able to offer a wide variety of products to a larger customer base at a lower price. Thus Weller began to pursue the Arts and Crafts ideal, "art for everyone."

Austrian born Rudolph Lorber helped push Weller pottery in the direction of molded artware. Hired in 1905, Lorber was soon charged with modeling new ceramic lines for the company. In 1910, Lorber designed the Ivory line. The reverence for nature of the Arts and Crafts and Art Nouveau movements clearly influenced Lorber's choice of subject matter when he designed the Forest, Woodcraft, Brighton, Muskota, Baldin, Flemish, and Zona lines. To get a sense of the range of items offered in such lines, the Woodcraft line (decorated with apple trees and their denizens...squirrels and owls) included ashtrays, candlesticks, comports, jardinières and stands, lamps, umbrella stands (which worked quite well for holding canes, integral fashion accessories for image conscious gentlemen and ladies through roughly the first quarter of the twentieth century), vases, and wall pockets. Rudolph Lorber would remain with the company until 1930 and additional lines will be discussed under in the Middle Years subheading.

Forest umbrella stand, stamped circular mark with Weller around the rim. 19.25" h. *Courtesy of Arnie Small and Barbara Gerr.* $2,135-2,350.

Woodcraft owl in tree trunk (apples and leaves on the back of the vase) vase and Woodcraft three foxes jardinière. Both are identified with an impressed "WELLER" mark. 13.25" h. vase and 7.5" d. jardinière. *Courtesy of Arnie Small and Barbara Gerr.* Vase: $2,280+. Jardinière: $300-400.

Woodcraft apple and leaves detail on the back of the owl vase. *Courtesy of Arnie Small and Barbara Gerr.*

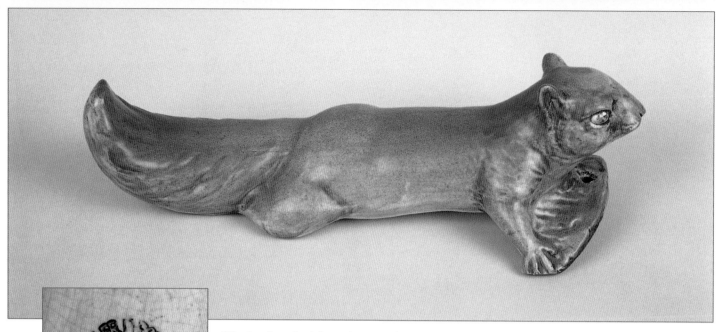

Woodcraft squirrel figure in natural
colors, meant to hang on the wall, ink
stamped mark with "Weller Pottery." 13"
h. *Courtesy of Arnie Small and Barbara
Gerr.* $1,540+.

Weller flower holder with two ducks. Unmarked. Either from the
Brighton or the Muskota line. 5.5". *Courtesy of Mark Mussio,
Cincinnati Art Galleries, LLC.* $200-300.

Muskota double chicks
figure, unmarked. 6.25" h.
*Courtesy of Arnie Small
and Barbara Gerr.* $780+.

Rudolph Lorber initialed and designed vase decorated with a sailing ship and sunrise, identified with an impressed "WELLER" mark. 8" h. *Courtesy of Arnie Small and Barbara Gerr.* NP.

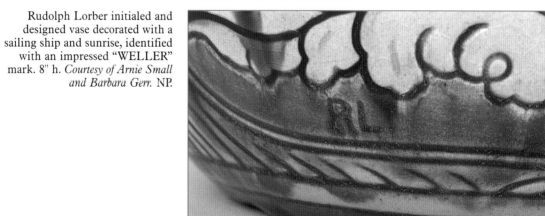

Flemish jardinière and pedestal with stylized four-petalled red and green flowers on an ivory ground. The pedestal measures 23.5" h.; the jardinière measures 13" x 15.5". *Courtesy of David Rago Auctions.* $500-750.

Zona pitcher with ducks splashing in puddles, stamped "Weller Pottery" mark. 7.5" x 7". *Courtesy of David Rago Auctions.* $200-300.

The Zona line used vividly rendered mold relief apples on the branch as its decorative motif. This design would later catch the eye of management at Gladding, McBean and Company in California. This West Coast firm would purchase the rights to the design for use in their Franciscan line. Renamed Apple, this line would be the first of several relief-molded designs in the Franciscan arsenal. It was also one of the longest lasting, as – at the time of this writing – Apple is still available, although now manufactured by an English conglomerate.

Two Zona 9.75" serving plates, each identified with an ink stamp mark. *Courtesy of David Rago Auctions.* $100-200.

The purchase of the design rights by Gladding, McBean did not keep Weller from using the Zona name, which appeared periodically on different lines, including the Zona Baby Ware, ceramics for the youngest set. Like many other potters, Weller also reintroduced once popular lines to a new generation of consumers under different line names and with alterations to glaze colors to match the preferences of the day.

Ending this early period, in 1917 the S. A. Weller Pottery Company created the Hudson line. This was an extremely popular line adorned with hand painted flowers and, at times, portraits and scenic views. The background glazing was blue and cream with a matt finish. Different background colors were used at times and given line names such as Hudson Perfecto or Rochelle. Hudson vases are frequently found signed by the artists.

Hudson vase with rose decoration by Sarah McLaughlin, front and back view with the McLaughlin signature on the lower left on the back, impressed "WELLER" mark. 14" h. *Courtesy of Ken and Sharon Ballentine.* $8,000-8,500.

Hudson Perfecto vase with apple blossoms encircling the vase, impressed "WELLER" mark in block letters. 4" h. *Courtesy of Mark Mussio, Cincinnati Art Galleries, LLC.* $300-500.

The Meaning Behind the Pot

To truly understand the ceramics produced by the S. A. Weller Pottery Company, one needs to understand how they were used and what they meant to the people who first purchased them. In 1895, when Weller introduced Louwelsa, the company was dealing with a Victorian society. Their wares reflect that in many ways.

Large Louwelsa vase with naturalistic treatment of grapes done, circa 1905, by Eugene Roberts. Clusters of red, black, and yellow grapes adorn the front of the vase with large vines wrapped by smaller ones below. Signed "E. Roberts" on the side near the base. 25" h. *Courtesy of Mark Mussio, Cincinnati Art Galleries, LLC.* $3,000-4,000.

Weller art pottery and artware was both useful and ornamental. In their decorative role, such ceramics displayed in homes stated that the family residing there was "genteel" – people of refinement and good taste. As will become evident below, this was of great importance to members of the Victorian middle class successful enough to strive to move into higher economic and social circles. It was also significant to those of the lesser means and recent immigrants. These people tended to be looked down upon by society at large. To counter perceptions that they were coarse and vulgar folk, individuals in these groups would purchase a few ornate objects from companies like Weller, proclaiming to all who observed them that gentility resided in this humble home as well. Neighbors visited each other far more frequently then than they do today. Among those who were not upwardly mobile, the presence of ornamental ceramics was a source of pride and dignity they shared during visits, bolstering them against the misperceptions of others they faced when away from the security of home and friends.

Victorians used flowerpots in and around their homes. Whether used in elegant conservatories or on humble windowsills and exterior staircases, decorative flowers and plants around the home were further evidence of cultural refinement. If the pots and jardinières were beautiful objects, so much the better.

Flowers were also seen as morally uplifting in the Victorian era. A homemaker might place flowering plants prominently around the home in the hope of elevating the morals of those she lived with. Medicinal herbs were also grown by some in flowerpots and planters, not only for their decorative value, but also for their use in homeopathic remedies. Some viewed these medicinal herbs as a sign of God's beneficence, providing natural cures for the children He loved and indirect evidence, through the cessation of pain, of an afterlife in which all pain was banished. When herbal remedies worked, they were perceived as a sign of God's very existence.

Flowers were once seen as morally uplifting. This garden pottery two-handled urn embossed with a wreath of laurel leaves under matte gray glazes can easily be imagined brimming with flowers. Identified with a stamped "WELLER WARE" mark. 15.5" x 13". *Courtesy of David Rago Auctions.* $250-350.

Different cultures ascribed different meanings to ornamental ceramics. While in Victorian American culture at large, such items were statements of refinement, to the Irish a cupboard full of ornamental objects spoke of other things. The Irish displayed the ceramics presented to them on important occasions, such as weddings, and those given to them by old friends and loved ones. To the Irish observer, that cabinet spoke of love and family history. No doubt those objects also launched many stories on quiet evenings when the day's work was done.

Public Demand, Public Desire

Driven by the engines of the Industrial Revolution, the Victorian age was a time of great social change. As previously stated, families migrated from rural to urban environments, from an agrarian to a technological society. Job opportunities and increased income flowed to a growing middle class, with men and women entering the labor pool together. Consumer buying power was on the rise. These forces created an ambitious middle class striving to climb both the social and economic ladders of success. Social functions, such as dinners, became formal and intricate affairs designed to impress those who could help you rise to new heights. And for the Victorians, to prove you were up-and-coming you needed things, lots of beautiful things. Art pottery wares were among those things Victorians turned to when proving their worth. Artful Weller ceramics could be found gracing the public rooms throughout a house, including the umbrella stand by the front door, comports, bowls, and flower arrangers on the table, vases in the niches, garden wares and pedestaled jardinières in the conservatories, figurines on the mantle, and candlesticks wherever they were needed.

Weller art pottery objects would have been proudly presented as gifts on birthdays, weddings, and other significant occasions. Such impressive items would have spoken well of the love the gift giver felt for the recipient and would have reflected equally well on the taste of the giver.

In Victorian society, after one of those socially significant formal dinners, gentlemen and their ladies separated. The ladies retired to the drawing room for coffee or tea and the gentlemen drank liquor and smoked, a practice they were not allowed to indulge in the presence of ladies. The host had his tobacco jar close at hand and well stocked with cigars. In those days, the cigar was a potent symbol of manly power and success. Weller produced a variety of intricate and amusing tobacco jars for just such occasions.

By the Victorian era, the woodland regions around developed areas were now "tamed," generally free of large carnivores or angry indigenous peoples. Victorians were free to view the relatively safe natural world around them with a romantic eye, rather than as the potential threat to life and limb it had been for their forebears. The Industrial Revolution also provided Victorians with greater access to the world at large than ever before. Explorers returned from around the globe with stories of exotic locales, flora, and fauna. All this led to a fascination with nature. This increasing interest in the natural world was reflected in the Arts and Crafts and Art Nouveau movements.

As an expression of this passion for nature, Victorians constructed elaborate gardens, hothouses, and indoor conservatories. Nature, well manicured, was ushered into the Victorian home. To accommodate this trend, potteries produced a wide range of garden accessories, from pedestaled jardinières and garden seats to elaborate planters, flower holders, and wall pockets.

A Word About Wall Pockets

Woodcraft or Flemish wall pocket measuring 9.5".
Courtesy of David Rago Auctions. $100-200.

In *American Art Pottery Wall Pockets*, Mark Bassett defines a wall pocket as "a vase made to hang on the wall." (2004, 4) Weller's first offering was an Art Nouveau (1904) line wall pocket shaped like a peacock feather. By 1916, dozens of different designs in these generally flat-backed ceramic objects designed to artfully display cut flowers or hanging plants were offered to Weller's customers. Plants well displayed in public rooms spoke well of a family's sophistication. Wall pockets provided another means to achieve that end. Bassett states wall pockets reached a zenith in popularity in 1916 when writer Clarence Moores Weed wrote of wall pockets in his "Garden and Orchard" column in *House Beautiful*. Weed suggested that they be hung in close association with Japanese art prints.

From the mid- to late nineteenth century, majolica wares with bright lead glazes that drew attention to themselves in dark and cluttered Victorian rooms had been all the rage. The Pennsylvania firm Griffen, Smith, & Hill had even designed a brightly colored majolica wall pocket in the shape of a butterfly in the 1880s. By contrast, Weed notes that the proper wall pocket of 1916 should not do such a thing (how Victorian that would be). He states, "... the eye of the observer should not be led away to the brilliance of the container." (Bassett 2004, 7) Times and tastes had changed.

Japanese design sensibilities had been introduced to the West via the South Kensington Exhibition of 1862, the Paris Exhibition of 1867, and Philadelphia's Centennial Exhibition in 1876. Intricate patterns covering every square inch of a vessel's surface gave way to the Japanese use of open space within designs. Such world's fair exhibitions of the nineteenth and early twentieth centuries provided the public with new ideas for decorating and design and fresh desires for new products in the same way that the popular television shows "Trading Spaces" and "While You Were Out" privately – and home, garden, and auto shows publicly – did for early twenty-first century consumers.

As the nineteenth century passed into the twentieth, the complexities of the Victorian age slowly gave way to a more casual form of living. In the nineteenth century, a Victorian man wearing a hat had to concern himself with when it was appropriate to tip or "doff" his chapeau. He was to tip his hat to his social equals, his betters, and to ladies. He doffed his hat to his banker but not his butcher. He was required to remove that hat when entering a residence but never in a place of business. In time, such arcane social rules became wearisome and gentlemen dropped them in favor of simply touching the brims of their hats with their fingers sociably when passing. Life became simpler.

The same trend occurred in ceramics. As the Victorian age passed, massive homes gave way to cheery bungalows; formal dinners requiring numerous courses and elaborate tableware were replaced by barbeques with limited place settings more appropriate to festive, casual dining.

Simplification was seen in ceramic shapes. Ornate forms with elaborate embellishments gave way to streamlined shapes and simple decorative techniques, a trend that would continue throughout the twentieth century.

Improved transportation technology was changing society as well during the nineteenth and twentieth centuries. Chain stores were becoming a rising power, meeting the needs of the less affluent amongst the middle and working classes ... and anyone keen on a bargain. It all began back just before Samuel A. Weller was born, around 1850, when the American clipper ships began dashing across the seas to China and back with loads of tea. In 1859, George F. Gilman and George Huntington Hartford began selling tea in a small shop on Vesey Street in New York City at a steep discount, roughly a third of the price anyone else was offering. They managed the feat by going straight to the clipper ships at the docks, both importing and purchasing tea in bulk from China and Japan straight off the boats, cutting out the middleman. Believing low prices were not enough, these two showmen did everything in their power to entice customers. Their shop sign featured large golden letters over a bright red background. The company name was a boast, The Great American Tea Company. Within the store, the cashier's cages were exotic Chinese pagodas, a large green parrot held center stage on the main floor, band music was offered on Saturdays, and premiums were given away to lucky customers. As their customer base grew, in 1863 the entrepreneurs added a widening range of low priced groceries to their offerings and had expanded their single store to a chain of six.

In 1869, once the Union Pacific Railroad successfully spanned the United States coast to coast, the Great American Tea Company changed its name to The Great Atlantic & Pacific Tea Company (the A & P for short) to capitalize on this exciting event. While this chain would not extend coast to coast until the 1930s, by 1912 there were almost five hundred A & P's and the concept of the chain store was well established. Chain stores worked well for traveling consumers. As Americans became increasingly mobile, these chain shops were familiar beacons for travelers in unfamiliar landscapes.

Increased mobility and improving transportation in the late nineteenth century also led to the rise of mail order catalog sales, a sales method Sears Roebuck and Company and Montgomery Ward both used to great advantage to reach customers in outlying regions with little access to large retail establishments. So successful was this system that by the middle of the twentieth century, Sears would be the largest general merchandise retailer in the United States. No doubt, manufacture of inexpensive artware was spurred, at least in part, by the growth of these powerful new outlets through which a potter could reach a broader consumer base.

As society transitioned out of the Victorian era, middle class consumers with fewer funds than aspirations were looking for art to enhance their homes and images without bankrupting themselves. Weller's molded, relief decorated artwares, economically produced, reasonably priced, and first introduced in 1905, were just the sort of things such consumers desired.

The Middle Period, 1918-1935

Of Artists and Their Wares

In 1920, Weller hired an expert in metallic luster glazes once again, this time as art director. John Lessell, born in Mettlach, Germany, had previously worked for the J.B. Owens pottery manufactory. At Weller, Lessell created the LaSa, Lamar, and Marengo metallic lusterwares, among others. These were labor-intensive glazes requiring as many as six different firings to complete. All three lines featured tall, artfully stylized trees in the foregrounds and various backgrounds including hills, lakes, and sweeping skies. Lessell is also credited with perfecting Weller's take on the famous Chinese red glaze with his Chengtu line. Chengtu items were glazed solid red with no additional hand decoration. John Lessell would leave Weller in 1925, and Henry Fuchs would take his place.

Tall LaSa baluster vase painted with gray trees in front of a gold, green, and red luster landscape, marked. 16" x 7".
Courtesy of David Rago Auctions. $400-600.

During this period, Rudolph Lorber continued to model impressive decorative artware lines including Glendale (c. 1928) and Coppertone (1929). Influenced by the Art Deco Movement, Lorber created the Hobart and Lavonia Art Deco lines in 1927.

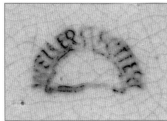

Coppertone vase with lily leaves, printed "Weller Pottery" with "half bottle kiln" mark. 11.5" h. *Courtesy of Arnie Small and Barbara Gerr.* $700+.

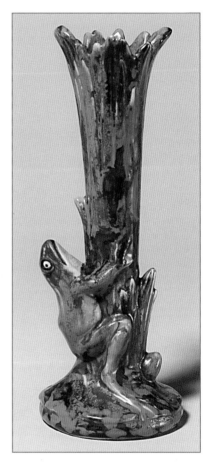

Coppertone bud vase with an ambitious frog climbing the side. Marked with a Weller semi-circular ink stamp. 9" h. *Courtesy of Mark Mussio, Cincinnati Art Galleries, LLC.* $800-1,000.

Working with Rudolph Lorber was Dorothy England Laughead, a Zanesville native, who modeled the Chase and Silvertone lines of the late 1920s. She also worked with Lorber on the Garden Animals line, featuring large animal figures intended for outdoor use.

Duck figure, possibly a garden piece, with "Weller Pottery" incised script mark. 11" h. *Courtesy of Arnie Small and Barbara Gerr.* $2,700+.

Additional popular artware lines produced by Weller in the 1920s included Blue Drapery, Glendale, Knifewood, Louella, and Warwick. The last of the hand-decorated lines would be Art Deco designs of the early 1930s, including Cretone, Geode, Raceme, and Stellar. By 1935, economic depression had brought an end to Weller's costly hand decoration. From that point forward, simple glazes and molded designs would suffice.

Center: Louella ruffled rim vase, 6.75" h.
Left: Klyro faceted bud vase decorated with flowering dogwood branch, 6.75" h.
Right: Baldin bottle-shaped vase, 6.75" h.
All are identified with an impressed "Weller" manufacturer's mark. *Courtesy of David Rago Auctions.* $150-250 each.

One of the lines produced during the 1930s seemed specifically designed to coax smiles from worried consumers struggling with limited finances. This was the Novelty Line, which included whimsical figures of dogs, kangaroos, monkeys, pigs, and wolves on ashtrays. Tumblers with faces were also offered. These cheerful items were produced in semi-gloss glazes.

The depression years beginning in 1929 brought the company opportunities as well as hardships. The S. A. Weller Pottery Company turned to the production of utility wares to increase sales. One example of Weller's utility ware was Light Blue Banded Ware, a white glazed cookware decorated with pinstripe lines on either side. While few depression era housewives were in the market for artware, all could still use a good solid casserole dish and a set of sturdy mixing bowls. The repeal of Prohibition offered Weller another "golden" opportunity, the chance to produce beer mugs. The company happily supplied this need for a society determined to make up for lost time.

Changes at the Top

In October 1925, Samuel A. Weller died. Harry Weller, Samuel's nephew, now took the reins of a company with several plants and hundreds of employees. Harry Weller would increase plant capacity by installing continuous kilns, which moved ceramics through the firing process on a conveyor belt passing through a tunnel kiln. The ware went in "green" (unfired) and came out fired hard and cooled at the other end. In 1931, the hard times of the Depression forced Harry Weller to reduce company operations down to a single plant. The following year, Harry Weller fell victim to an automobile accident. Following Harry Weller's death, the leadership of S. A. Weller Pottery would pass through Samuel A. Weller's sons-in-law, Frederic Grant, Irvin Smith, and Walter M. Hughes.

Public Demand, Public Desire

During the 1920s, America recovered from the effects of the First World War, finding new and exciting diversions, entertainments, machinery, and nightclubs to pursue. Radios sold by the millions and brought the world home. Henry Ford made it possible to move out en masse into that world, once listeners' radio shows were finished. Prior to World War I, the automobile was unattainable by most. After the war, Ford's assembly line approach to auto manufacturing produced cars nearly everyone could afford. This new-found mobility would move people out of cities to newly established suburbs in droves, send them traveling back to town for shopping, movies featuring Charlie Chaplin, Buster Keaton, and Tom Mix, and to speakeasies. During the Prohibition era from 1919 until the early 1930s, speakeasies attracted large crowds for music, dance, and illegal beer, gin, and whiskey. These were the "Roaring Twenties," and consumers were looking for artware that reflected the bright and exciting times they were living in; yet, artware that was not too expensive, mind you, as these consumers had a great many things they wished to spend their money on.

However, factories in the "Roaring Twenties" had been producing goods in great volume, yet paying workers too little to make them good consumers. Farmers who had needed loans to keep up with record demands for crops during World War I were faced with declining needs for their produce in the 1920s and discovered they could not easily pay their debts. An extended drought in the American Midwest worsened their problems. Further, during the giddy years of the 1920s, many speculated in the New York stock market, seeking a quick and easy road to riches. By 1929, the economy slowed, the stock market crashed, and economic depression hit the nation hard. By 1932, twelve million Americans would be out of work. Thousands would lose their homes; millions would seek out charities for basic necessities.

Consumers were finding life difficult at best in the 1930s and pared back their expectations. An article in the trade journal *Ceramic Industry* dated May 1935 summed up the needs and desires of consumers during the Depression years.

The author interestingly attributed the elimination of formal dining in favor of informal table sets to the repeal of Prohibition rather than to economic hardship. Desired dishes and accessories were to be colorful as well as informal.

The depressed economy created a "drab atmosphere" that housewives sought to relieve with bright and cheerful color schemes for the home, including lively artware for inspiration.

Finally, the consumer of 1935 was seeking wares in soft pastel shades that would emulate the drapes and furniture home decorators were promoting.

By the middle years of the 1930s, businesses were slowly recovering from the effects of the Depression and were rehiring workers. The federal government took steps to protect workers and promote unions. Federal programs were put into place to protect farmers and homeowners as well. The situation facing potters at the beginning of 1935 was encouraging, according to *Ceramic Industry*:

> Stores in the New York area on one Saturday during the [Christmas] holiday season did the largest single day's volume sale on china and glassware since 1931 …

Having weathered the Depression, this was the situation facing the S. A. Weller Pottery Company as it headed into its final years.

The Late Period, 1935-1948

Of Artists and Their Wares

After hand decoration ceased in 1935, Weller produced two new, inexpensive single fired lines a year. For these lines, bisque body and glaze were fired together in a single, economical operation. Decorative emphasis was placed on molded body form and innovative glazes. The Cactus line was one example of the new, inexpensive lines. Cactus animal figurines were molded, glazed, and fired once. These lines worked nicely for Weller during the lean years.

Dorothy England Laughead would continue to produce intriguing designs during these final Weller years. One striking example is the Ollas Water Bottle (*see Snyder 1999, p. 173 for an example of this bottle*). Once you have seen it, the Ollas is not easily forgotten. It is shaped like a gourd, the upper end and stem forming the lid.

The undertray upon which the gourd rests features relief molded leaves on the surface. These water bottles were trimmed in various glaze colors on the undertray and upper half of the bottle. There was a trick to this design. The thick ceramic body was allowed to remain semi-porous. This allowed the water bottle to sweat, keeping the bottle and its contents cooler on a hot summer's day.

Among the later lines produced by Weller were Arcadia, Atlas, Panella, Pastel, and Roba. Arcadia features a cream matt glaze finish, scalloped rims, and relief molded flowers and leaves adorning the body. The Atlas line featured angular, star-shaped bodies glazed in several colors. Some of the Panella forms were handled and all were decorated with relief molded nasturtiums and leaves. The Pastel line featured simple, modern shapes glazed in pastel colors, the colors *Ceramic Industry* had reported consumers were seeking in 1935. The Roba line was decorated with draped flowers and leaves and glazed in various matt finish colors.

Atlas light yellow squat vessel marked "Weller C-3". 4" x 6".
Courtesy of David Rago Auctions. $200-300.

Foreign competition was an increasing worry for American pottery firms. The imports were well produced and less expensive than the domestic product. Consumers were finding these imported wares increasingly attractive. However, in 1935, the manager of a large department store declared that he was now "... among those in favor of the development of a home pottery industry and style trends to end price competition [with foreign imports]. With the exceptionally fine designers whom domestic potters have enrolled there is every incentive now to carry on a style competition for the domestic trade." (*Ceramic Industry* January 1935, 10)

In 1940, the famous designer Russel Wright would do just that. Wright organized a program entitled American Way. His intent was to give American modern design the same kind of attention and boost that world's fairs had always offered manufacturers. The best of American design and manufacturing was to be displayed in the most prominent department stores of the day. This was intended to be an impressive event. In fact, Eleanor Roosevelt extended the invitation to the opening at Macy's in New York on September 21, 1940.

Wright's criteria for a sound modern design included:

> a practical form that is comfortable and efficient; materials employed that have the surface, weight, and strength to withstand the demands placed upon them through regular use; manufacturing that is economical, efficient, and produces objects with balance, durability, and security. (Kerr 1998, 287-288)

These were to be original American designs, not items derivative of European design, as had been common practice for many manufacturers. Wright hoped that with proper exposure to these modern designs, American homemakers would be convinced to purchase American made items instead of those inexpensive products imported from overseas.

The S. A. Weller Pottery Company contributed to the American Way display with leaf, grape, and melon bowls and leaf and spiral vases, all glazed in Turkish red and turquoise. In September 1941, *Ceramic Industry* declared, "One of the outstanding designs among the American Way pieces was a series made by Weller Potteries."

The State of the Industry

Pottery firms found a new outlet for their wares in the late 1930s. Theaters began offering ceramic and glass items to moviegoers on a regular basis. In an unusual marketing ploy in 1937, the *New Yorker* magazine purchased 7,800 candlesticks from the Fulper Pottery Company in Colonial Blue. To these they added a phrase from Shakespeare, "How far that little candle throws his beam." The finished products were delivered to the magazine's advertisers and agencies to promote the *New Yorker*. Who knows what unusual uses Weller ceramics were put to that will come to light as the years go by?

During the 1930s, pottery manufacturers were increasingly frustrated by foreign competition in their home market. They felt the American public was biased in favor of overseas goods, not just for price considerations, but also out of a deep-seated belief that domestic products were inferior. That was an image American potters had been battling since 1876. It was felt that American merchants held the same bias.

In 1937, Frederick H. Rhead, by then the art director for the Homer Laughlin China Company, reported on the state of affairs overseas. What Rhead observed was no comfort to the American potting industry. At the Paris Exposition, Rhead observed, "... the ceramic and other craft works, particularly those shown by Italy, Sweden, and Denmark, are very fine." From there, he moved on to Florence and Milan, Italy, and toured two pottery works, "... the former producing very beautiful porcelain and artwares and the latter, equipped with tunnel kilns and an elaborate system of conveyors concentrating on mass production approaching that of any American factory." (*Ceramic Industry* September 1937) Many in the American industry saw World War II as an opportunity to make inroads into the domestic market while the foreign trade was cut off.

The Second World War also created a number of challenges for the American pottery industry. The availability of raw materials was unpredictable; workers were scarce. Some companies took to hiring high school boys part time after school to handle general maintenance and janitorial work around the pottery plants. The Selective Service and munitions plants took many of the available workers. While women had been working in Ohio potteries since the nineteenth century, predominantly in decorating departments, pottery factories took additional steps to accommodate greater numbers of women in their work force. Fuel shortages were always a worry. Transportation for wares produced was limited and far from reliable.

During the war years, pottery companies were forced to cut back on production. They culled out the slow selling wares, offering lines reduced to their best sellers of years past, at times featuring different glazes or decorations. Little in the way of new shapes and decorative treatments were produced during the war, particularly as most plants were now turning at least part of their production over to war materials commissioned by the national government.

Of the artware industry, the *Bulletin of the American Ceramic Society* reported:

> The combined production of art and garden pottery achieved a total of 5.7 million dollars in 1939.

Although no exact data are available, the 1943 volume undoubtedly was much larger owing to greater demand, cessation of imports, and relative freedom from materials shortages. In California, there has been a marked increase in the number of whiteware plants in recent years, almost all of which are engaged in the production of artware and ceramic novelties of various types. The California producers, though small operators in many cases, are producing artware of first quality, both ceramically and artistically. They have done much to educate the public to the merits of American-made ceramic ware and have gained for domestic producers a large part of the artware market formerly monopolized by European producers. Based on shipments of raw materials to the artware industry, it is estimated that the 1943 output of art and garden pottery totaled 14.3 million dollars, a great increase over the 1939 figure. Postwar sales will vary directly with the national income and should remain at the level of at least 10 million dollars in the immediate postwar period, even allowing for some resumption of imports. (Newcomb 1945, 49)

During the war, hardware stores had trouble stocking their shelves with metal products due to wartime restrictions. To fill the space, store managers turned to artware, along with china, glass, and mirrors.

Public Demand, Public Desire

As the world moved toward war, worried Americans sought some small relief in whimsical ceramic figurines and other novelty items. By 1940, ceramic miniatures were found to be attractive as well, ranging from tiny dishes, lamps, and candles to diminutive animals.

As the world moved toward war, worried Americans sought some small relief in whimsical ceramic figurines and other novelty items. Mammy cookie jar, 1935, marked in script "Weller Pottery Since 1872." 11.5" x 7". *Courtesy of David Rago Auctions.* $1,250-1,750. This smiling figure holding a watermelon was part of the company's Decorated Novelty Utility Line introduced in 1935 to help meet the public's desire for whimsy in uncertain times. Accompanying the cookie jar in this line were a syrup and teapot (each with a mammy at the top), creamer, sugar, and batter bowl (the sugar sported two black children caricatures as handles, while the creamer and batter bowl each featured a single child figural handle). This mammy was not merely cheerful, however. She also assured consumers that the cookies inside would be fine. During the early decades of the twentieth century, the stereotypical mammy figure was associated with quality food products.

As the nation plunged into battle, Victor Schreckengost, the famous designer working with the American Limoges and Salem China potteries, noted a change in style and design brought about by the advent of war:

> It looks as if we are returning to the sentimental, dainty and more colorful styles and decorations, as exemplified by the eighteenth century school of design. This is a direct influence of the war. In such periods people discover that they have hearts after all, and they yearn for the things that harmonize with their emotions. For the duration of the war, the eighteenth century influence will be predominant in practically all household furnishings. (Gibney 1942, 36)

The End of a Company

Although the S. A. Weller Pottery Company survived the Great Depression and continued potting during the war years, the effort had taken a toll and 1945 found the firm struggling financially. Foreign ceramics returned to the marketplace and Weller could not adequately compete. Weller's president, Walter M. Hughes, leased dormant factory space to the Essex Wire Corporation in 1945. By 1947, Essex Wire had purchased enough Weller stock to control the company. In 1948, pottery manufacturing ceased.

Weller Ceramics A-Z

Here is a rapid reference to many of the most popular wares produced by Weller, organized alphabetically by line name. When the date provided beside the line name is by period (early, middle, or late period), this is a general listing denoting that this line was in production at some point during this period. It does not suggest that the line so noted was produced throughout that entire period. See the Appendix for a listing of all the lines currently known to have been produced by Weller.

It is quite possible that some of the dates or date ranges provided for the lines will change over time as additional research refines our knowledge. Some lines may even move from one period to another. This is to be expected in any field where active research is conducted and is basic to the nature of any scholarly pursuit.

Ardsley pillow vase with orchids, marked with printed "Weller Ware" and "half kiln" mark. 7.75" h. *Courtesy of Arnie Small and Barbara Gerr.* $300+.

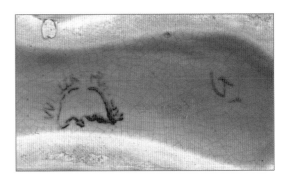

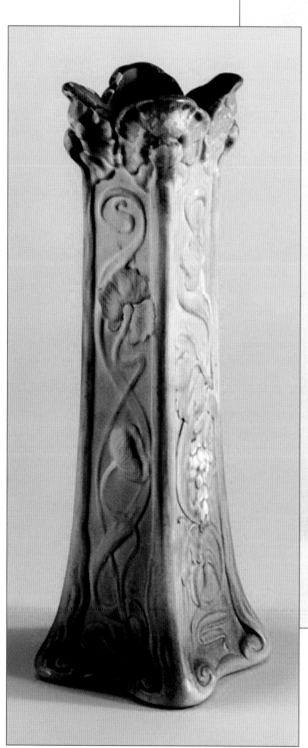

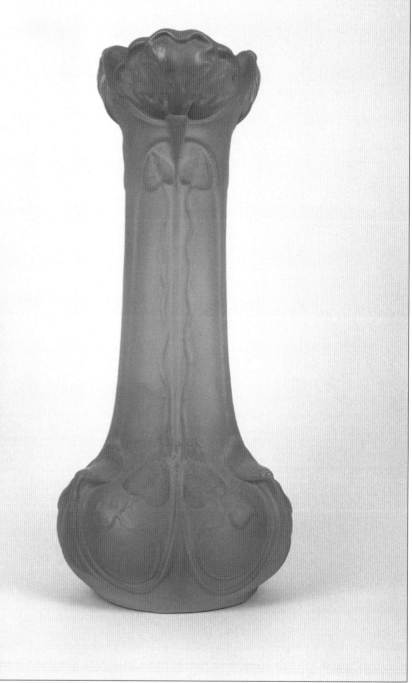

L'Art Nouveau matt glaze vase with poppies, unmarked. 11" h. *Courtesy of Arnie Small and Barbara Gerr.* $300-400.

L'Art Nouveau four-sided vase with panels of poppies and grapes, unmarked. 11" x 3.25". *Courtesy of David Rago Auctions.* $300-400.

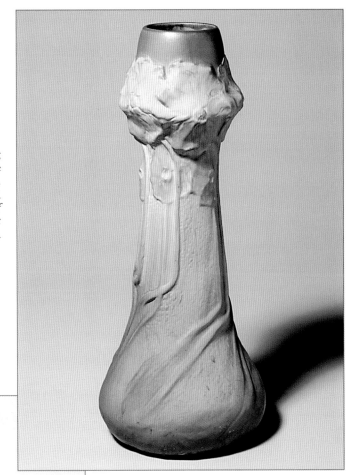

L'Art Nouveau vase showing poppies on elongated stems, done in pastel shades of pink and green. Marked "WELLER" in small block letters. 13.75" h. *Courtesy of Mark Mussio, Cincinnati Art Galleries, LLC.* $400-600.

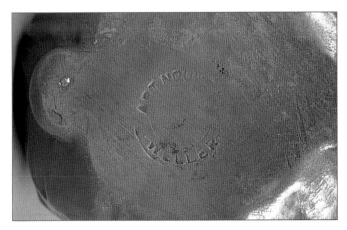

Art Nouveau corn vase in copper glaze, identified with an impressed "Art Nouveau Weller" circular mark. 9.75" h. *Courtesy of Arnie Small and Barbara Gerr.* $270-300.

Atlas, late period (1935-1948)

Atlas flaring star-shaped bowl in blue and ivory, marked.
6" x 9.25". *Courtesy of David Rago Auctions.* $150-250.

Aurelian, 1898-1910

Aurelian twisted, faceted
vase painted with
carnations, identified
with an etched mark.
7.5" x 6". *Courtesy of
David Rago Auctions.*
$250-350.

Aurelian vase on three feet decorated in yellow carnations. Incised "Weller Aurelian" and impressed "68 7" marks. 4.25" h. *Courtesy of Mark Mussio, Cincinnati Art Galleries, LLC.* $200-300.

Aurelian whiskey jug with grape decoration by Frank Ferrell. Signed with the artist's monogram on the side. Incised "Aurelian Weller K" and stamped "380 6" marks on the base. 6" h. *Courtesy of Mark Mussio, Cincinnati Art Galleries, LLC.* $300-400.

Aurelian jug decorated with golden cherries and green leaves on a gold-to-brown background, painted by Helen Windle, whose initials are on the jug's front. Marks include impressed block lettered "WELLER," impressed numbers "279" and "8", and the line name "Aurelian" incised into the base. 5" h. *Courtesy of Mark Mussio, Cincinnati Art Galleries, LLC.* $300-400.

Aurelian mug, decorated with plums, leaves, and branches by Charles Chilcote. Marks include the "Aurelian Weller" logo, the incised number "435", and the artist's signature on the side of the mug. 6.5" h. *Courtesy of Mark Mussio, Cincinnati Art Galleries, LLC.* $200-250.

Aurelian mug decorated with blackberries. The artist, possibly Minnie Mitchell, has created a natural array of life-sized berries and leaves. Marks include the "Aurelian Weller" logo and an impressed "562" as well as artist's initials on the side of the mug. 6" h. *Courtesy of Mark Mussio, Cincinnati Art Galleries, LLC.* $150-200.

Aurelian ewer with a graceful, sweeping handle and wild roses decoration by Marie Rauchfuss. Marks include the "Aurelian Weller" logo, an impressed "605", and the slip-painted initials of the artist on the surface. 9" h. *Courtesy of Mark Mussio, Cincinnati Art Galleries, LLC.* $300-400.

Auroro: a.k.a. Aurora, Auroral, c. 1904

Rare Auroro ovoid vase painted with a single brown blossom, marked. 6.5". *Courtesy of David Rago Auctions.* $700-900.

Auroro vase with daisies on a pale blue ground, marked "Weller" in script. 8" x 4". *Courtesy of David Rago Auctions.* $650-950.

Baldin, middle period (1918-1935)

Baldin squat vase identified with a "WELLER" stamped mark. 5.5" x 7". *Courtesy of David Rago Auctions.* $200+.

71

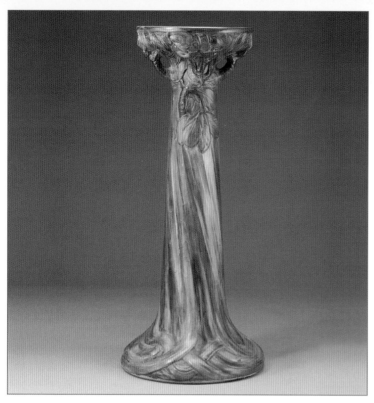

Tall Baldin pedestal, unmarked. 27" h.
Courtesy of David Rago Auctions. $500+.

Brown Baldin umbrella stand, unmarked. 22" h.
Courtesy of David Rago Auctions. $600+.

Three Baldin vases, one with a glossy glaze, two
include manufacturer's marks. 7" and 9.5" h.
Courtesy of David Rago Auctions. $300+ each.

Brown Baldin large squat vase, unmarked. 7" x 10".
Courtesy of David Rago Auctions. $300+.

Two brown Baldin bulbous vases, one marked. 6" each.
Courtesy of David Rago Auctions. $300+ each.

Two blue Baldin vases: a corseted vase in pale
blue and a planter, unmarked. 10" and 6".
Courtesy of David Rago Auctions. $300+ each.

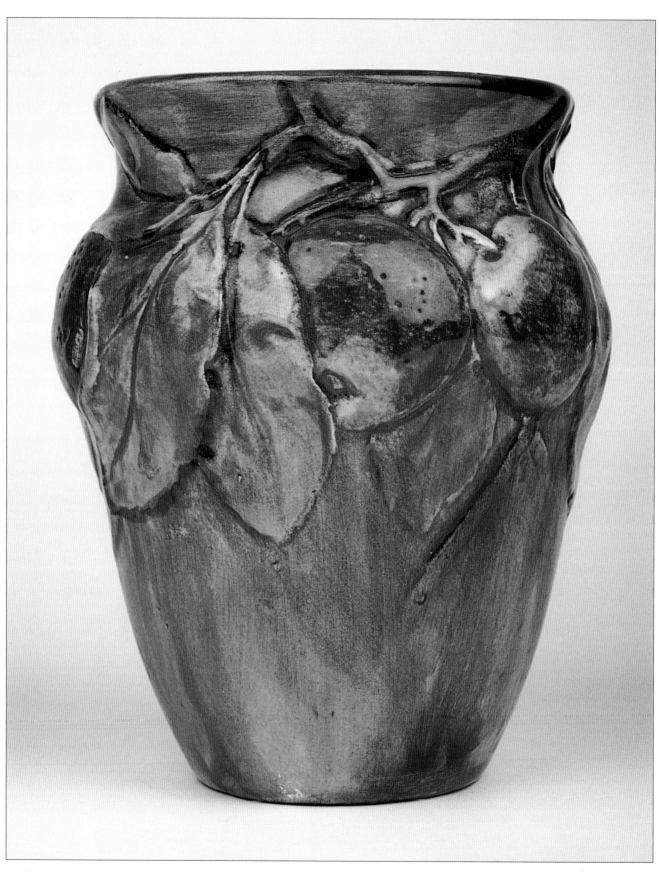

Baldin vase with embossed apple decoration and impressed
"WELLER" mark. 7.25" h. *Courtesy of Bob Shores and Dale Jones.* Values
for Baldin vases have been found to vary widely across the country.
Values as high as $750 or more for a vase have been found in some areas.

Barcelona vase with a faint gold manufacturer's mark on the base. 18" h. *Courtesy of Ken and Sharon Ballentine.* $850-1,000.

Barcelona hand-painted vase with three "handles", unmarked. 10"
h. *Courtesy of Arnie Small and Barbara Gerr.* $400-450.

Barcelona three handled vases. The larger vase has a paper label (used during the 1930s and 1940s) and a faint gold maker's mark; the smaller vase also has the gold mark. 14" and 10" h. *Courtesy of Ken and Sharon Ballentine.* 14" vase: $600-700; 10" vase: $400-450.

Three Barcelona vases with twisted handles. The largest vase has a paper label and black "Weller/Barcelona" stamp; the center vase has a black "Weller/Barcelona" stamp; the smallest vase has a gold stamp mark. 11", 8", and 6.5" h. *Courtesy of Ken and Sharon Ballentine.* 11" vase: $400-450; 8" vase: $325-375; 6.5" vase: $250-275.

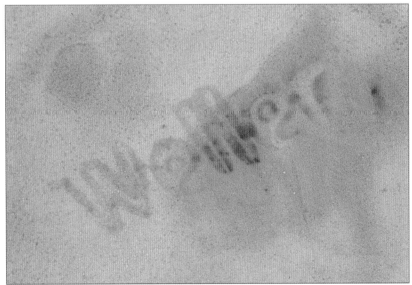

Barcelona vase identified with a printed "Weller" mark. 10" h.
Courtesy of Ken and Sharon Ballentine. $450-500.

Barcelona vase identified with a paper label and gold "Weller"
mark. 9" h. *Courtesy of Ken and Sharon Ballentine.* $300-350.

Barcelona jardinière identified with a gold printed "Weller" mark. 9" h. *Courtesy of Ken and Sharon Ballentine.* $350-400.

Three Barcelona ewers. The ewer on the left has a gold stamp mark. The center ewer has a black "Weller" stamp and a partial paper label. The ewer on the right has a gold "Weller" stamp. 6", 6", and 9" h. *Courtesy of Ken and Sharon Ballentine.* Left to right: $225-250; $250-275; $350-400.

Barcelona pitcher with spout, gold stamp maker's mark.
10" h. *Courtesy of Ken and Sharon Ballentine.* $350-400.

Three handled Barcelona jars. The jar on the left has a paper label; the center jar is marked with a "Weller Barcelona" ink stamp; the jar on the right has a gold stamp. 9.5", 6", and 7" h. *Courtesy of Ken and Sharon Ballentine.* Left to right: 9.5" jar: $300-325; 6" jar: $175-200; 7" jar: $200-225.

Three handled Barcelona jars. The jar on the left has a gold stamp mark; the center jar is marked with a black "Weller" stamp; and the jar on the right is marked with a gold stamp. 9.5", 6.5", and 7.5" h. *Courtesy of Ken and Sharon Ballentine.* Left to right: 9.5" jar: $300-350; 6.5" jar: $225-250; 7.5" jar: $250-275.

Three handled Barcelona jars. Left: black "Weller Barcelona" stamp; center and right: gold stamps. 9.5", 7", 7.5" h. *Courtesy of Ken and Sharon Ballentine.* Left to right: 9.5" jar: $325-375; 7" jar: $250-275; 7.5" jar: $300-325.

Barcelona ewer identified with a
black stamped "WELLER"
mark. 12" h. *Courtesy of Ken and
Sharon Ballentine.* $475-550.

Barcelona handled pot with a printed "WELLER" manufacturer's mark. 6" h. *Courtesy of Ken and Sharon Ballentine.* $175-200.

Barcelona bowl identified on the base with a faint manufacturer's
mark. 8" d. *Courtesy of Ken and Sharon Ballentine.* $150-175.

Barcelona bowl identified with a gold printed Weller mark and paper label. 7" h. *Courtesy of Ken and Sharon Ballentine.* $150-175.

Barcelona cup, printed
"WELLER BARCELONA"
mark. 7" h. *Courtesy of Ken and
Sharon Ballentine.* $225-275.

Barcelona tall chambersticks. 8.5" h. *Courtesy of Ken and Sharon Ballentine.* $700-800 pair.

Barcelona candlesticks with a printed "WELLER / BARCELONA" manufacturer's mark. 2" h. *Courtesy of Ken and Sharon Ballentine.* $225-275 pair.

Blue Drapery: a.k.a. Drapery, c. 1920

Drapery jardinière and pedestal, unmarked. The
pedestal measures 18.5" h.; the jardinière measures 10.5"
h. *Courtesy of David Rago Auctions.* $300-500.

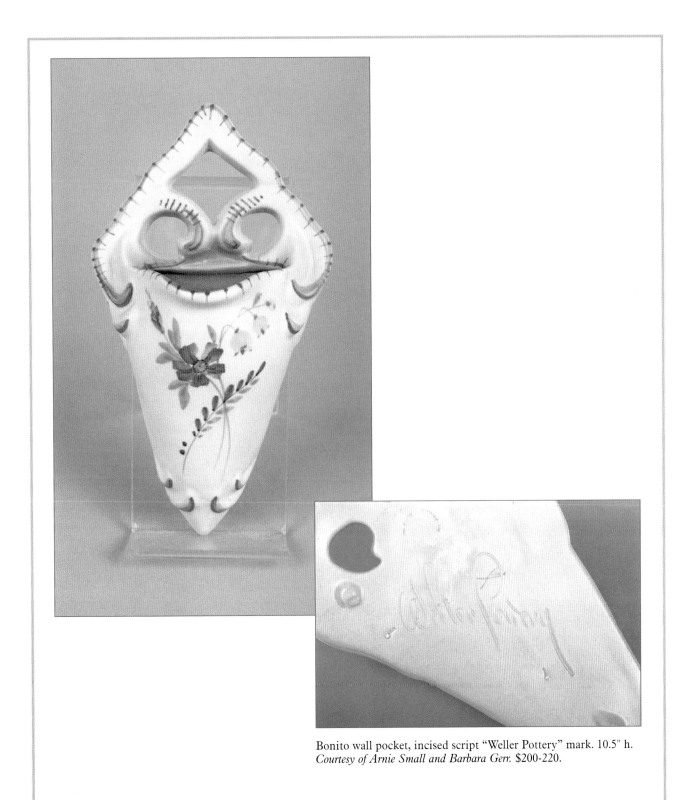

Bonito wall pocket, incised script "Weller Pottery" mark. 10.5" h.
Courtesy of Arnie Small and Barbara Gerr. $200-220.

Bonito ovoid two-handled vase painted with pink and amber
columbine, marked "Weller Pottery" in script. 11" x 5.5".
Courtesy of David Rago Auctions. $225-275.

Brighton colorful parrot figure on an ornate stand, unmarked except for hand written "12" on the base. 8" h. *Courtesy of Arnie Small and Barbara Gerr.* $840-925.

Brighton tall parrot figure on an ornate curving stand, impressed "WELLER" mark with "PE" on the base. 12.75" h. *Courtesy of Arnie Small and Barbara Gerr.* $840-925.

Brighton, two small bird flower frogs, unmarked. 3.75" h. *Courtesy of Arnie Small and Barbara Gerr.* $450+.

Two examples of Brighton kingfishers on perches with varying glazes in natural colors. The left hand example has a paper label underneath reading "From the White Pillars Museum." Both measure approximately 9" high. *Courtesy of Arnie Small and Barbara Gerr.* $390+ each.

Bronze Ware, middle period (1918-1935)

Bronze Ware tall baluster vase, unmarked. 13.75" x 7".
Courtesy of David Rago Auctions. $400-600.

Burnt Wood, c. 1910

Burnt Wood vase featuring the three Wise Men on camels heading across the desert. Unmarked. 15.5" h. *Courtesy of Mark Mussio, Cincinnati Art Galleries, LLC.* $400-600.

Cameo Jewel: a.k.a. Cameo Jewell, Jewell, 1910-1920

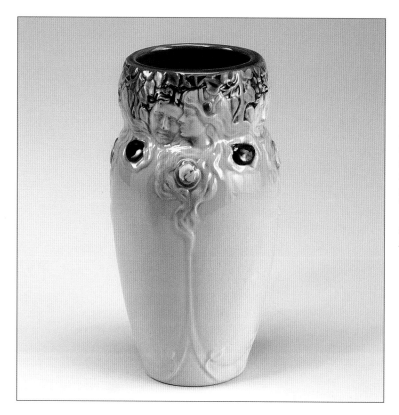

Rare Jewell vase embossed with images of a man and woman around the rim, identified with an impressed "WELLER" mark. 10.75" x 5.5". *Courtesy of David Rago Auctions.* $900-1,250.

Chase, late period (1935-1948)

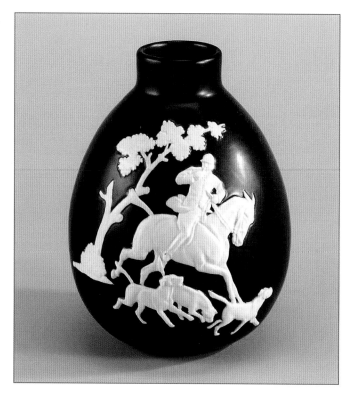

Chase bulbous vase identified with a "Weller Pottery" script mark. 10" x 7.25". *Courtesy of David Rago Auctions.* $450-650.

Clarmont vase with impressed "WELLER" mark and printed "3,"
c. 1920. 7.25" h. Molded flower around rim and molded vertical
lines on stem and horizontal lines above and below. Brown glaze
with black wash. *Courtesy of Bob Shores and Dale Jones.* $250-275.

Claywood
The date of release is uncertain as sources range from c. 1910 to the middle period (1918-1935).

Claywood vases decorated with panels of flowers, unmarked.
3.5" x 3.25". *Courtesy of David Rago Auctions.* $150-250.

Claywood corseted vase with pine cones, identified
with an impressed "WELLER" mark. 6.5" x 4.25".
Courtesy of David Rago Auctions. $200-300.

Coppertone, middle period (1918-1935)

Coppertone large flaring bowl, identified with a paper label (used during the 1930s & '40s) and "SS." 3" x 11.25". *Courtesy of David Rago Auctions.* $300-400.

Coppertone bowl with flower frog, marked. 15" x 10". *Courtesy of David Rago Auctions.* $750-950.

Coppertone beaker-shaped vase, marked "Weller" in script. 5.75" x 5". *Courtesy of David Rago Auctions.* $300-400.

Coppertone tall corseted vase with an incised "Weller Handmade" mark. 12.5" h. *Courtesy of David Rago Auctions.* $500-750.

Coppertone flaring vase marked "Weller Hand-made".
13.5" x 6". *Courtesy of David Rago Auctions.* $500-700.

Coppertone beaker-shaped vase incised with the letter "Z."
6" h. *Courtesy of David Rago Auctions.* $250-350.

Short Coppertone vase. 5" h. *Courtesy of Arnie Small and Barbara Gerr.* $330-440.

Coppertone frog figurine, kiln stamped manufacturer's mark. 2.5" x 2.25". *Courtesy of David Rago Auctions.* $220-330.

Coppertone frog figurine stamped "Weller Pottery." 2.5" x 2.25".
Courtesy of David Rago Auctions. $220-330.

Coppertone frog figurine marked
with incised and inked "Weller
Pottery" in script. 4" h x 3" l.
Weller's figurines have ceramic
eyes. *Courtesy of Arnie Small and
Barbara Gerr.* $600-660.

Coppertone frog figure with hole in mouth marked with a printed "Weller Pottery" mark. 5.5" h. x 6" l. *Courtesy of Arnie Small and Barbara Gerr.* $825-900.

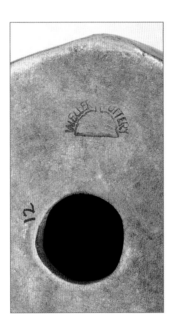

Coppertone turtle figure. 6.5" l. *Courtesy of Arnie Small and Barbara Gerr.* $720-790.

A pair of Coppertone candlestick holders with turtle and lily
pad, marked. 3.25" h. *Courtesy of David Rago Auctions.* $350-500.

Coppertone bowl with perched frog and lily pads, marked with a half-kiln maker's mark. 2" x 15".
Courtesy of David Rago Auctions. $500-700. In a 5.5" x 9.75" size, this bowl is valued $750-1,000.

Coppertone bowl with frog and lily pad, marked "WELLER POTTERY."
15" x 10.5". *Courtesy of David Rago Auctions.* $400-600.

Coppertone console bowl with flower flog, frog and lily pad design, marked with printed "Weller Pottery," "MD," and "19" marks. 14" long. *Courtesy of Arnie Small and Barbara Gerr.* $400-600.

Coppertone frog and flower console bowl with central flower frog, printed "Weller Ware" mark with bottle kiln. 10.5" l. *Courtesy of Arnie Small and Barbara Gerr.* $400-600.

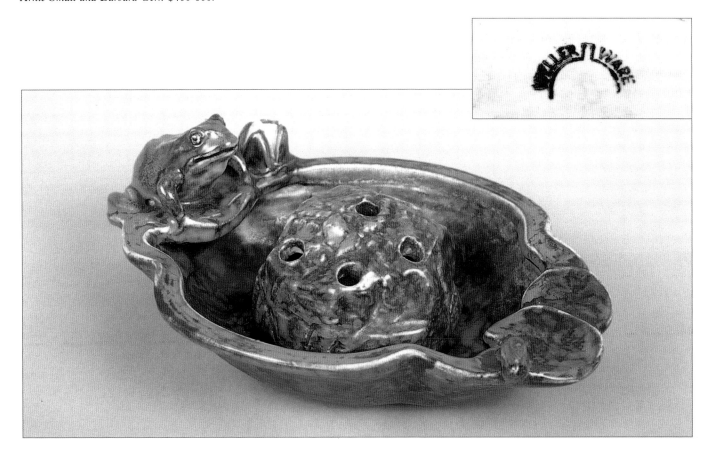

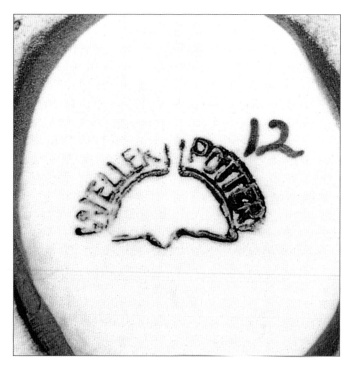

Larger bowl in Coppertone with frog perched on one end, printed "Weller Pottery" mark. A large fish design is molded into the side of the bowl but is rather difficult to see beneath the glaze. 10.5" l. x 5" h. *Courtesy of Arnie Small and Barbara Gerr.* $500+.

Coppertone frog and flower dish, unmarked. 4" x 5".
Courtesy of David Rago Auctions. $150-250.

Rare Coppertone flaring vase with tall lily pad and trefoil decoration on body, four frogs' heads surround the base. This vase is identified with the half-kiln manufacturer's mark. 11.25" x 5.5".
Courtesy of David Rago Auctions. $1,925-2,200.

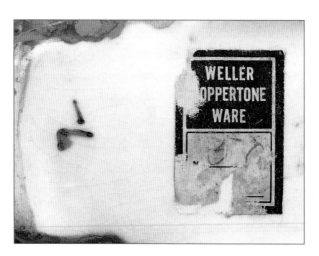

Coppertone fan vase with frogs and a paper label reading "Weller Coppertone Ware." 8" h. *Courtesy of Arnie Small and Barbara Gerr.* $1,780-1,960.

Coppertone double fish vase marked with printed "Weller Pottery" and bottle kiln maker's mark. 8" h., *Courtesy of Arnie Small and Barbara Gerr.* $3,300+.

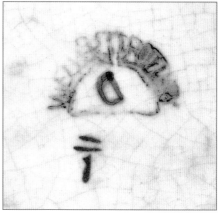

Coppertone jardinière with a climbing frog on the outside, identified with a printed "Weller Pottery" maker's mark. 7" h. to frog's nose. *Courtesy of Arnie Small and Barbara Gerr.* $1,440+.

Coppertone jardinière with two frogs, identified with an inked "Weller Pottery" with bottle kiln maker's mark. 7" h. *Courtesy of Arnie Small and Barbara Gerr.* $2,050+.

Copra, 1915

Copra jardinière and
pedestal adorned with
tulips. The jardinière is
identified on the base
with a stamped
"WELLER"
manufacturer's mark.
*Courtesy of David Rago
Auctions.* $300-420.

Creamware, 1915-1930

Creamware lidded tobacco
jar embossed with pipes,
pouches, and flowers,
unmarked. 7.5" x 5.5".
*Courtesy of David Rago
Auctions.* $150-250.

Cretone, c. 1934

Cretone bulbous vase with black flowers, leaves, and gazelles on a cream ground, identified with a "Weller Pottery" script mark and artist's initials "MT". 6.75" x 7". *Courtesy of David Rago Auctions.* $350-500.

Dickens Ware I (First Line), 1897-1898
Dickens Ware II (Second Line), 1898-1905
Dickens Ware III (Third Line), 1905

Dickens Ware I jardinière painted with nasturtiums on a dark green ground, identified with an impressed manufacturer's mark and an artist's cipher. 11.5" x 7.5". *Courtesy of David Rago Auctions.* $300-400.

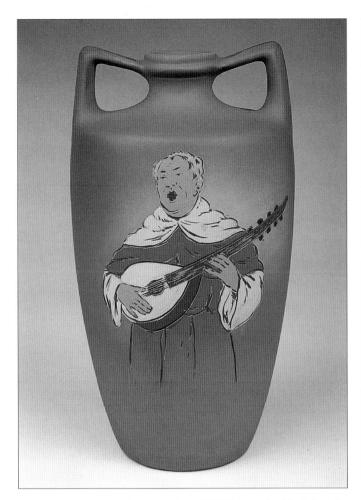

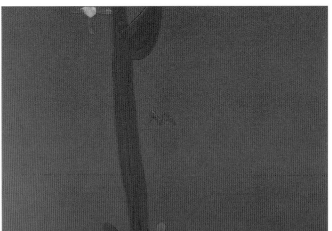

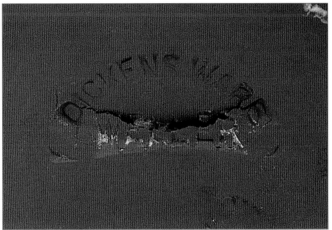

Dickens Ware II handled vase, signed "VA" for artist Virginia Adams, and identified on the base with an impressed "Dickens Ware Weller" mark. 10" h. *Courtesy of Ken and Sharon Ballentine.* $800-900.

Dickens Ware II vase with portrait of a monk playing a flute, decorated by Anna Best and signed by her on the side. Marked "Dickens Ware Weller" and "602 1" on the base. 10" h. *Courtesy of Mark Mussio, Cincinnati Art Galleries, LLC.* $400-600.

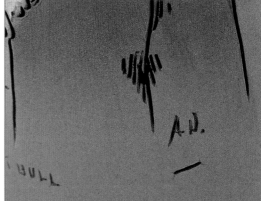

Dickens Ware II vase, decorated with the image of a Native American identified as "Ghost Bull" by Anna Dautherty and signed with her initials. The vase is identified with an impressed "Dickens Ware Weller" mark. *Courtesy of Ken and Sharon Ballentine.* $2,700-3,000.

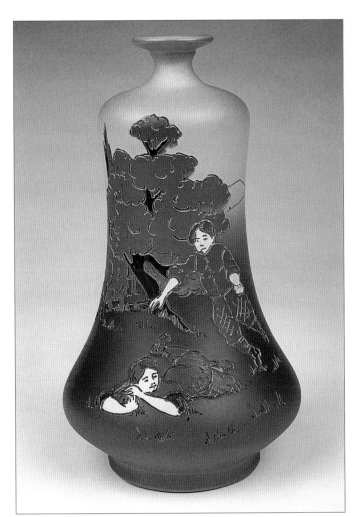

Dickens Ware II vase by
Anna Dautherty (who
initialed her art "A D"),
identified with an impressed
"Dickens Ware Weller" mark
on the base. 9" h. *Courtesy of
Ken and Sharon Ballentine.*
$1,900-2,200.

Dickens Ware II vase by Anna Dautherty,
identified on the base with an impressed
"Dickens Ware Weller" mark. 9.5" h.
Courtesy of Ken and Sharon Ballentine.
$3,200-3,500.

Dickens Ware II vase decorated by Anthony Dunlavy, impressed "Dickens Ware Weller" maker's mark on the base. 12" h. *Courtesy of Ken and Sharon Ballentine.* $2,300-2,600.

Dickens Ware II handled vase, artist signed "BH", and identified with an incised "Dickens Weller" maker's mark. 14" h. *Courtesy of Ken and Sharon Ballentine.* $2,200-3,000.

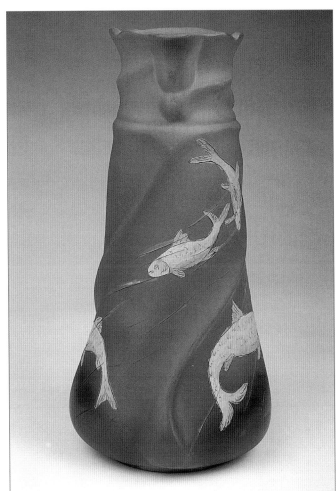

Dickens Ware II tankard
decorated by Edwin L. Pickens
(with Weller Pottery from 1904-
1920s, working on Dickens Ware,
Eocean, and Perfecto) and signed
"E.L. Pickens", no
manufacturer's mark. 11.5" h.
*Courtesy of Ken and Sharon
Ballentine.* $1,800-2,000.

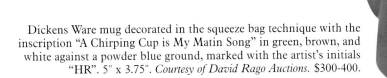

Dickens Ware mug decorated in the squeeze bag technique with the
inscription "A Chirping Cup is My Matin Song" in green, brown, and
white against a powder blue ground, marked with the artist's initials
"HR". 5" x 3.75". *Courtesy of David Rago Auctions.* $300-400.

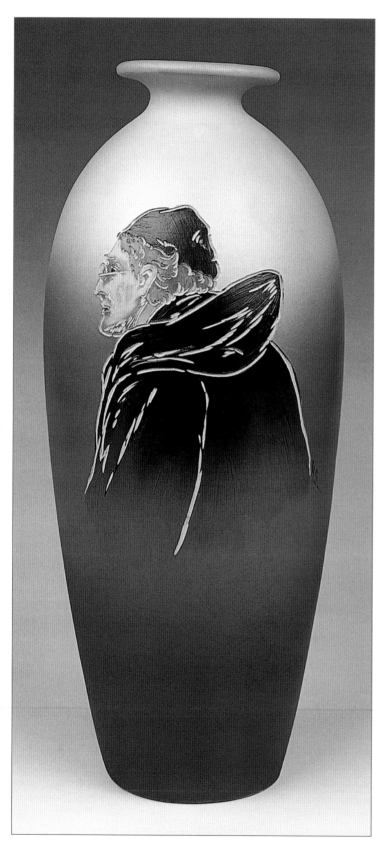

White-bodied Dickens Ware II. The base clay is white, which is unusual. The decoration is by Helen Smith, who marked her work with her initials "HS", marked on the base "X / 345". 15" h. *Courtesy of Ken and Sharon Ballentine.* $3,500-4,000.

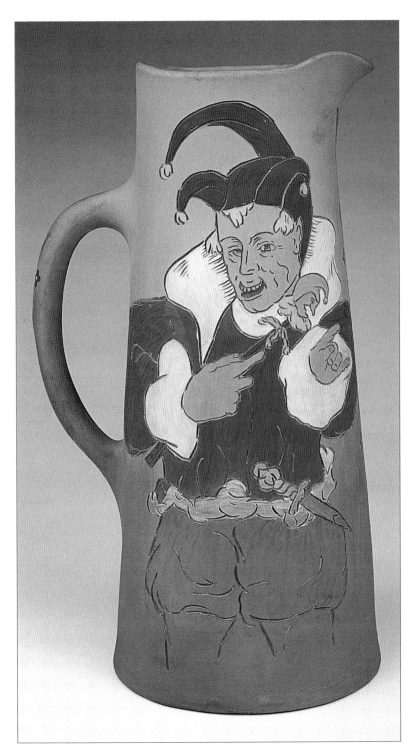

Dickens Ware II tankard decorated by Helen Smith (incised "HS" on the base), identified with an impressed "Dickens Ware Weller" maker's mark. 12" h. *Courtesy of Ken and Sharon Ballentine.* $2,700-3,000.

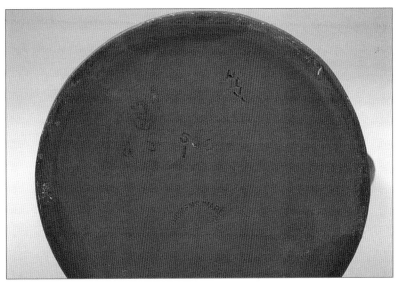

Dickens Ware vase, blue on blue, decorated by Helen Smith and identified with her "HS" initials. 16" h. *Courtesy of Ken and Sharon Ballentine.* $2,200-2,500.

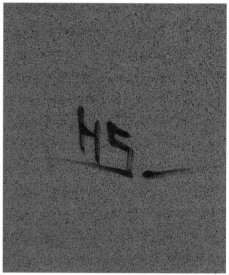

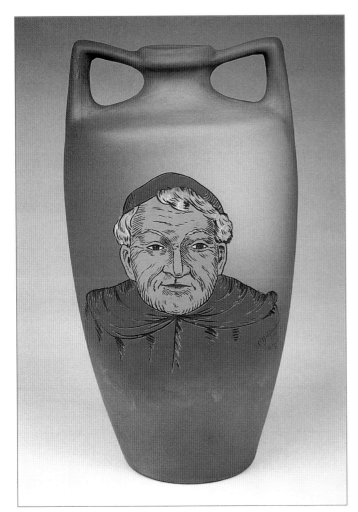

Dickens Ware II vase, dated 1901 and double signed "C. B. Upjohn" and "Gordon Mull". 10" h. *Courtesy of Ken and Sharon Ballentine.* $1,800-2,000.

Dickens Ware vase, blue on blue, marked with the initials "M. Y." 18" h. *Courtesy of Ken and Sharon Ballentine.* $2,500-2,800.

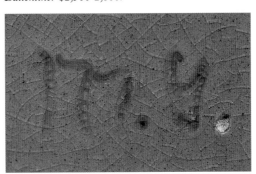

Dickens Ware II tall pitcher with a dolphin spout and handle,
incised with a swimming carp decorated in a polychrome glaze on
a green ground, marked "Dickens Ware Weller 328." 13" x 6.5".
Courtesy of David Rago Auctions. $650-950.

Dickens Ware II three-sided vase incised with
swimming fish, identified with an impressed mark.
6.25" x 4.5". *Courtesy of David Rago Auctions.* $385-500.

Dickens Ware II vase, not signed by an artist, marked "Dickens Ware Weller" on the base. 16" h. *Courtesy of Ken and Sharon Ballentine.* $7,000-8,000.

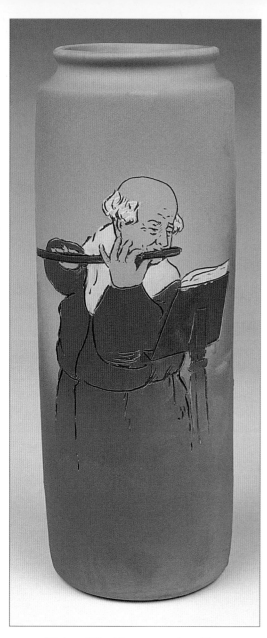

Dickens Ware II handled vase, identified with an impressed "Dickens Ware Weller" manufacturer's mark. 5.5" h. *Courtesy of Ken and Sharon Ballentine.* $400-500.

Dickens Ware II vase, not signed by an artist, identified with an impressed "Dickens Ware Weller" manufacturer's mark. 10.5" h. *Courtesy of Ken and Sharon Ballentine.* $900-1,000.

Dickens Ware II vase, no artist's signature, identified with an impressed "Dickens Ware Weller" manufacturer's mark. 10" h. *Courtesy of Ken and Sharon Ballentine.* $700-800.

Dresden Ware: a.k.a. Holland

Dating disparity exists here, with sources indicating production dates ranging from 1905-1909 to the middle period (1918-1935).

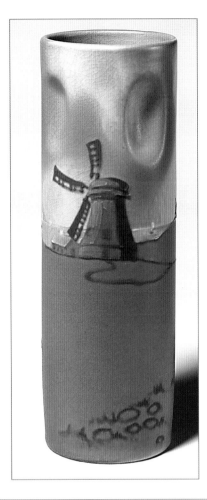

Dresden cylinder-shaped vase with a scene of the Dutch countryside in mat blues and greens, decorated by Levi Burgess. Marks include the incised notation "Weller Matt L.J.B" and impressed "9072". 10" h. *Courtesy of Mark Mussio, Cincinnati Art Galleries, LLC.* $500-700.

Eocean: a.k.a. Late Eocean, Eosian, and Eocean Rose, 1898-1915

Eocean is an early art pottery line featuring a white clay body adorned with underglaze slip decoration featuring imagery from the natural world, including animals, birds, fish, and flowers, along with character studies, all over a background in light blue, brown, or gray. Eocean Rose features background glaze colors in shades ranging from rose to gray.

Eocean ovoid vase painted with gooseberries and leaves, identified with an etched "Eocean Weller X164" mark. 10.5" x 3.75". *Courtesy of David Rago Auctions.* $300-400.

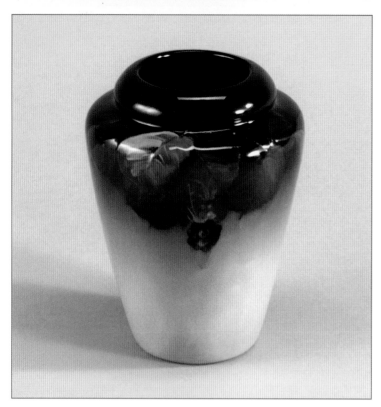 

Eocean vase with flat shoulder and cupped rim, painted with red berries and leaves, marked with an etched "Eocean Weller X522." 7.25" x 5.25". *Courtesy of David Rago Auctions.* $300-400.

Eocean cylindrical vase painted with berries and leaves, identified with a stamped maker's mark. 9.75" x 4.25". *Courtesy of David Rago Auctions.* $200-300.

Eocean ovoid vase painted with cherries, identified with a stamped "WELLER" manufacturer's mark. 9" x 4". *Courtesy of David Rago Auctions.* $200-300.

Eocean pitcher decorated with ripe cherries and leaves sprouting from a bough. Marked "Weller 9046" on the base; two incised Xs are also present. 6.25" h. *Courtesy of Mark Mussio, Cincinnati Art Galleries, LLC.* $300-400.

Eocean vase decorated with roses. Marks include incised "Weller Eocean," "FX," "8," and the initials of the decorator, "WG," painted on the side. 7" h. *Courtesy of Mark Mussio, Cincinnati Art Galleries, LLC.* $400-500.

Large and rare Late Eocean lamp vase with two blue birds perched on a crabapple bough, decorated by an unknown artist. The form has factory cast holes in the bottom and on the side for wiring, proving the original intent of the piece was to act as a lamp component. Marked "Arthur Powell" in the bottom. Cincinnati Art Galleries states, "... we believe Powell may have been a potter or finisher at Weller." 15.25" h. *Courtesy of Mark Mussio, Cincinnati Art Galleries, LLC.* $2,000-3,000.

Late Eocean vase with yellow irises and accented with dark pink on a gray to black ground. Unmarked. 8" h. *Courtesy of Mark Mussio, Cincinnati Art Galleries, LLC.* $300-400.

Etched Floral incised tankard decorated and signed by Frank Ferrell, identified with a hand-printed "WELLER" manufacturer's mark. 12" h. *Courtesy of Ken and Sharon Ballentine.* $2,900-3,200.

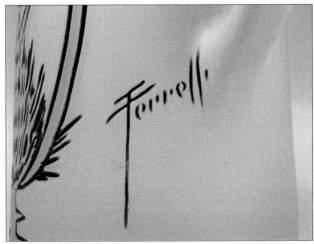

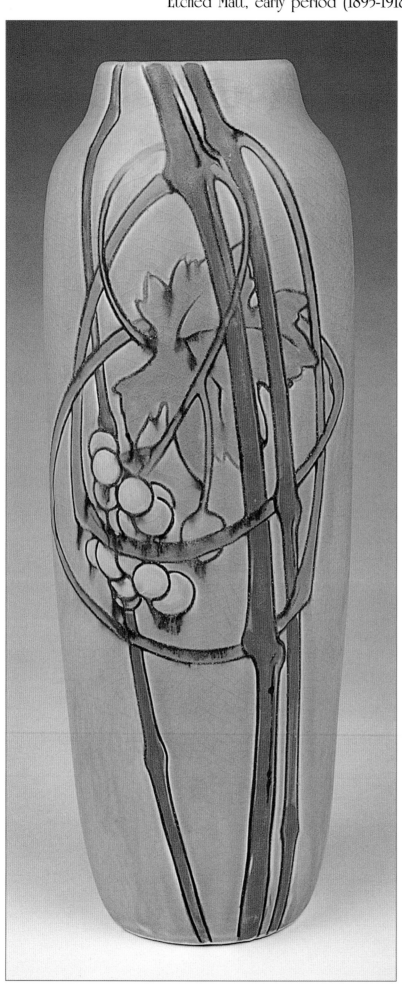

Modeled Etched Matt vase, not signed by an artist, identified with an impressed "WELLER" manufacturer's mark. 13" h. *Courtesy of Ken and Sharon Ballentine.* $900-1,100.

Etched Matt jardinière by Frank Ferrell with a band of sunflowers in burnt orange on ivory over a celadon ground, includes the artist's signature. 10" x 13.5". *Courtesy of David Rago Auctions.* $440+.

Etched Matt jardinière and pedestal decorated with stylized sunflowers designed by Frank Ferrell. Bands of sunflowers encircle the jardinière and pedestal with all etching outlined in black. Signed "Ferrell" on the side of the jardinière, otherwise unmarked. 31.25" h. *Courtesy of Mark Mussio, Cincinnati Art Galleries, LLC.* $2,000-3,000.

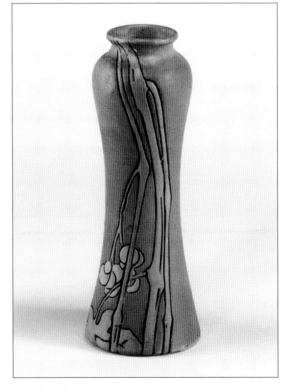

Modeled Etched Matt corseted vase with a stamped manufacturer's mark. 10.75" x 4". *Courtesy of David Rago Auctions.* $400-600.

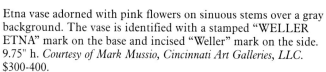

Etna vase adorned with pink flowers on sinuous stems over a gray background. The vase is identified with a stamped "WELLER ETNA" mark on the base and incised "Weller" mark on the side. 9.75" h. *Courtesy of Mark Mussio, Cincinnati Art Galleries, LLC.* $300-400.

Etna corseted vase painted with pink poppy, identified with an impressed mark. 10" x 3.5". *Courtesy of David Rago Auctions.* $250-350.

Etna vase painted with pink colored, molded phlox on a shaded gray ground. Marked "Weller Etna" on the base and impressed "Weller" on the side. 11" h. *Courtesy of Mark Mussio, Cincinnati Art Galleries, LLC.* $200-300.

Etna squat vessel with two crossed handles, slip-decorated with pink blossoms, stamped maker's mark. 4.75" x 8.75". *Courtesy of David Rago Auctions.* $200-300.

Etna classically-shaped vase painted with pink roses, identified with a stamped "WELLER ETNA" mark. 10.25" x 4". *Courtesy of David Rago Auctions.* $200-300.

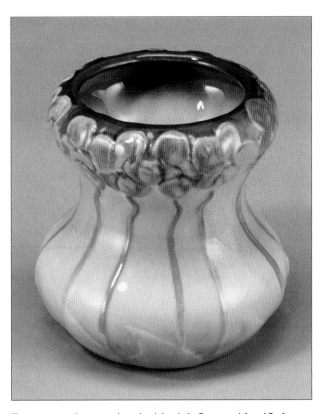

Etna corseted vase painted with pink flowers, identified with a stamped "Weller Etna" mark. 4.5" x 3.75". *Courtesy of David Rago Auctions.* $150-250.

Etna vase showing a large pink poppy on a shaded green ground. Marked "Weller" both on the side and on the base. 10" h. *Courtesy of Mark Mussio, Cincinnati Art Galleries, LLC.* $100-150.

Etna vase decorated with fairly stylized red wild roses with green leaves over a shaded gray background. Impressed "Weller Etna" mark. 5.5" h. *Courtesy of Mark Mussio, Cincinnati Art Galleries, LLC.* $70-100.

Flemish umbrella stand with swags of ivy over women holding wreaths of dogwood, unmarked. 20" x 10". *Courtesy of David Rago Auctions.* $1,200+.

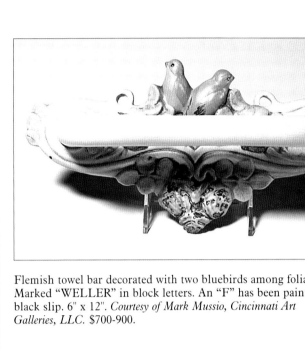

Flemish towel bar decorated with two bluebirds among foliage. Marked "WELLER" in block letters. An "F" has been painted in black slip. 6" x 12". *Courtesy of Mark Mussio, Cincinnati Art Galleries, LLC.* $700-900.

Flemish planter with band of leaves and fruit, unmarked. 10.5" x 12". *Courtesy of David Rago Auctions.* $200-300.

Flemish bowl decorated with trees and birds on a wire, unmarked. 3.75" x 8". *Courtesy of David Rago Auctions.* $100-200.

Fleron, middle period (1918-1935)

Fleron bulbous vase with mottled pink interior, marked "Weller Ware/Hand Made" in ink. 8.25" x 5.25". *Courtesy of David Rago Auctions.* $100-200.

Florala, c. 1915-20

Florala cylindrical vase with molded flower and geometric decoration, blue "WELLER" printed mark, c. 1915-20. 9.5" h. *Courtesy of Bob Shores and Dale Jones.* $250.

Floretta, 1904

Matt Floretta tankard with pear decoration, initialed by artist "B.L." below the handle. Cincinnati Art Galleries states, "Typically seen with apples, this is a variation of Second Line Dickens Ware which is generally marked "Floretta" on the bottom, as is this piece, along with an incised Weller and the notation X 264." 13" h. *Courtesy of Mark Mussio, Cincinnati Art Galleries, LLC.* $400-500.

Forest, middle period (1918-1935)

Forest jardinière and pedestal, the only mark is a hand-printed "T" on the base of the jardinière. Jardinière: 11" h., 12.5" d.; pedestal: 17.75" h. *Courtesy of Arnie Small and Barbara Gerr.* $1,440-1,585.

Forest hanging basket,
no mark, base also
decorated. 9.5" d.
*Courtesy of Arnie Small
and Barbara Gerr.*
$450-500.

Forest hanging basket, unmarked. 7.75" d. *Courtesy of David Rago Auctions.* $250+.

Forest pitcher, in high glaze naturalistic shades of brown, green, and blue, depicting trees, a stream, and the sky. Marked "WELLER" in block letters. *Courtesy of Mark Mussio, Cincinnati Art Galleries, LLC.* $200-300.

Frosted Matt, middle period (1918-1935)

Frosted Matt lamp base with a factory drill hole (the hole was subsequently widened by a later owner) covered in a blue feathered glaze, unmarked. 9" x 4.5". *Courtesy of David Rago Auctions.* $250-350.

Rare Fru-Russett vase embossed with a salamander and covered in a veined raspberry matte glaze, identified with a "WELLER" stamped manufacturer's mark. 4.75" x 3". *Courtesy of David Rago Auctions.* $500-750.

Fru-Russett gourd-shaped, two-handled vase embossed with green leaves on a blue and rose ground, stamped "WELLER." 6" x 6". *Courtesy of David Rago Auctions.* $600-900.

Fudzi, c. 1906

Fudzi vase with elaborate poppy decoration by Gazo Fudji. The artist incised flowers, stems, and leaves and added pinpricks to enhance his work. The design was then colored with rich enamels. Unmarked. 11.75" h. *Courtesy of Mark Mussio, Cincinnati Art Galleries, LLC.* $1,500-2,000.

Garden Ware, middle to late periods
(1918-1935; 1935-1948)
A variety of garden ornaments and figures.

Comical hen and chicks (part of garden ornament series) marked in incised script "Weller Pottery" (like comic dog). 8" h. *Courtesy of Arnie Small and Barbara Gerr.* $2,050+.

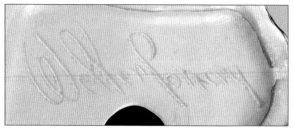

Glendale, middle period (1918-1935)

Glendale large ovoid vase, identified with a stamped
"WELLER WARE" manufacturer's mark. 13.25" x 5.5".
Courtesy of David Rago Auctions. $600-900.

Glendale ovoid vase, unmarked. 8.25" x 4.5".
Courtesy of David Rago Auctions. $540-780.

Glendale console set including a
large, flaring console bowl, a
flower frog, and a pair of low
candlesticks, identified with a
Weller kiln mark. Centerbowl:
15.5" d. *Courtesy of David Rago
Auctions.* $480-720 set.

Greenaways, 1900-1910

Rare Greenaways floor vase decorated with hand-painted landscapes with windmills, identified on the base with an incised "S.A. Weller" manufacturer's mark. *22" x 11". Courtesy of David Rago Auctions.* $1,500-2,000.

Greora, middle period (1918-1935)

Greora flaring vase marked "Weller Pottery" in script. 11.5" x 6.25". *Courtesy of David Rago Auctions.* $300-400.

Greora vase with flared rim, unmarked. 6.5" x 5.25". *Courtesy of David Rago Auctions.* $250+.

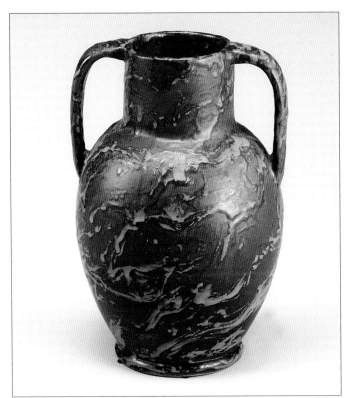

Greora bulbous two-
handled vase, marked
"Weller Pottery" in script.
10" x 6.5". *Courtesy of David
Rago Auctions.* $400-600.

Greora bulbous vase, incised "G." 5" x 4".
Courtesy of David Rago Auctions. $150-250.

Greora covered jar, identified with an incised
"Weller Pottery" mark in script. 6.25" x 5".
Courtesy of David Rago Auctions. $450-650.

Greora flaring bowl, marked.
2.5" x 14.5". *Courtesy of David
Rago Auctions.* $400-500.

Hobart, c. 1928

Hobart bud vase with a figure of a woman holding her dress,
covered in a green-blue glaze, identified with a stamped mark.
11" x 8". *Courtesy of David Rago Auctions.* $200-300.

Hudson, 1917-1934
Artists would continue to sign Hudson wares until 1934.

Hudson vase painted by Ruth
Axline with multicolored apple
blossoms on a shaded, deep blue
background. Marked with the
semi-circular Weller ink stamp
manufacturer's mark, an "A" is
painted on the base in black slip,
and the artist's last name is painted
on the foot of the vase. 7" h.
*Courtesy of Mark Mussio, Cincinnati
Art Galleries, LLC.* $300-400.

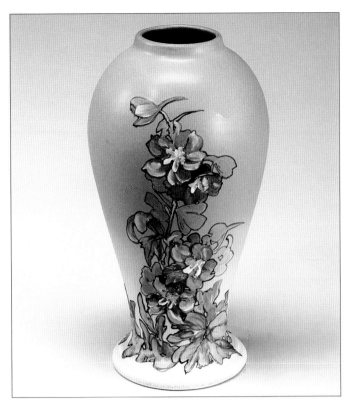

Hudson vase painted by Dorothy England with blue delphiniums, marked "D. England", kiln stamp "WELLER" manufacturer's mark. 12.5" x 6". *Courtesy of David Rago Auctions.* $350-450.

Hudson Perfecto vase decorated by Dorothy England with watercolor style blue and lavender iris decoration. Marked "WELLER" in block letters and signed by Dorothy England at the base. 7.25" h. *Courtesy of Mark Mussio, Cincinnati Art Galleries, LLC.* $300-400.

Hudson baluster vase painted by Dorothy England with blue
Freesia, marked with a full-kiln stamp manufacturer's mark. 8.25"
x 3.5". *Courtesy of David Rago Auctions.* $300-400.

Hudson bulbous vase painted by Dorothy England Laughead (and
initialed with her "D. L." mark) with pink poppies on a shaded
gray to pink ground. Marked "Weller" in script. 10.5" x 5".
Courtesy of David Rago Auctions. $350-450.

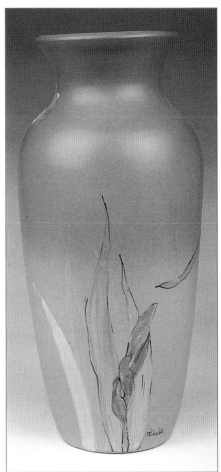

Hudson Floral vase by Sarah McLaughlin, signed by the artist near the base, "Weller Pottery" incised script manufacturer's mark. 15" h. *Courtesy of Ken and Sharon Ballentine.* $3,800-4,200.

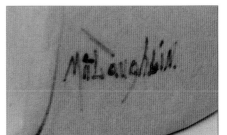

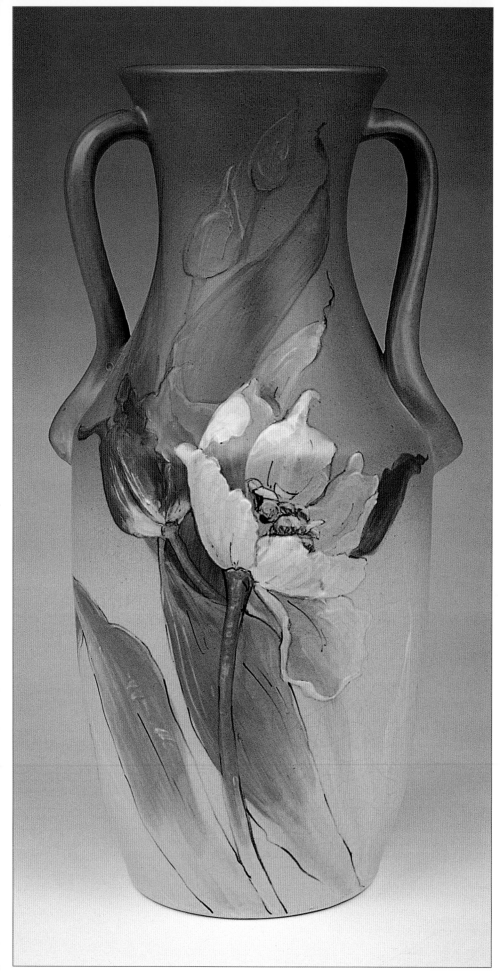

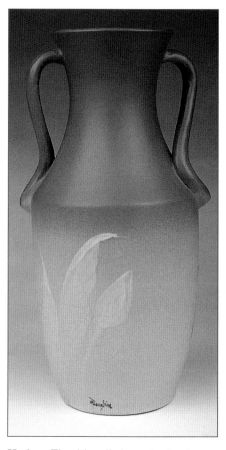

Hudson Floral handled vase by Sarah McLaughlin, front and back, "Weller Pottery" incised script manufacturer's mark. 15.5" h. *Courtesy of Ken and Sharon Ballentine.* $5,500-6,000.

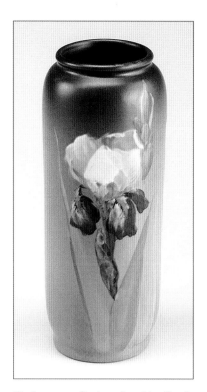

Hudson vase painted by Sarah McLaughlin with blue and white irises on a blue ground, identified with an incised "Weller Potter" manufacturer's mark and an artist's cipher. 15" x 7". *Courtesy of David Rago Auctions.* $3,000+.

Hudson vase finely painted by Sarah McLaughlin with an iris on a shaded blue ground, identified with an impressed "WELLER" maker's mark and the artist's signature. 9.5" x 4". *Courtesy of David Rago Auctions.* $1,200+.

Hudson vase decorated and signed by Hester Pillsbury, with many white and pink hollyhocks on a blue to pink ground. The flowers have been outlined in black. Marks include the artist's signature on the vase's side and a "Weller" ink stamp manufacturer's mark on the base. 12" h. *Courtesy of Mark Mussio, Cincinnati Art Galleries, LLC.* $800-1,000.

Hudson ovoid vase finely painted by Hester Pillsbury with violets. This vase is marked with a "WELLER" ink stamp manufacturer's mark. 10" x 4". *Courtesy of David Rago Auctions.* $500-750.

Hudson vase decorated by Hester Pillsbury with white and blue Morning Glories, nicely accented with pink. Marked "WELLER" in block letters on the base and signed by the artist on the side. 8" h. *Courtesy of Mark Mussio, Cincinnati Art Galleries, LLC.* $500-700.

Hudson Perfecto bulbous vase by Hester Pillsbury, painted with apple blossoms on a crazed white to blue ground, identified with an impressed "Weller" maker's mark and the artist's initials. 6" x 5". *Courtesy of David Rago Auctions.* $300-400.

Hudson bulbous vase painted by Hester Pillsbury with wild roses, identified with a "full kiln" ink stamp manufacturer's mark and the artist's mark. 9" x 4.5". *Courtesy of David Rago Auctions.* $450-650.

Hudson Floral vase decorated by Mae Timberlake, and signed "Timberlake" at the base by the artist. No manufacturer's mark. 15" h. *Courtesy of Ken and Sharon Ballentine.* $3,900-4,300.

Hudson vase with lotus blossoms, buds, and leaves on a shaded blue ground, decorated by artist Mae Timberlake and signed on the side. Impressed "Weller Pottery" on the base. 7.75" h. *Courtesy of Mark Mussio, Cincinnati Art Galleries, LLC.* $400-600.

Hudson vase displaying white prunus blossoms with black leaves and branches on a tan ground, decorated by Mae Timberlake. The vase is marked "Weller Ware" with an ink stamp manufacturer's mark and has the artist's name signed at the base. 7.75" h. *Courtesy of Mark Mussio, Cincinnati Art Galleries, LLC.* $400-600.

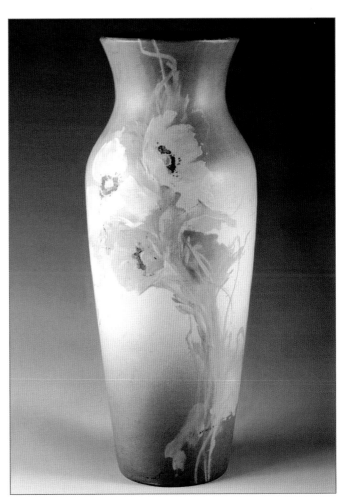

Hudson vase with flaring rim, painted by Sarah Timberlake with blossoms in polychrome. This vase is marked with an ink stamped "WELLER" maker's mark, kiln stamp, and artist's mark. 7" x 3". *Courtesy of David Rago Auctions.* $250-350.

Rare Hudson floor vase decorated with poppies in pastel tones, stamped "WELLER." 22.5" x 9". *Courtesy of David Rago Auctions.* $2,500-3,500.

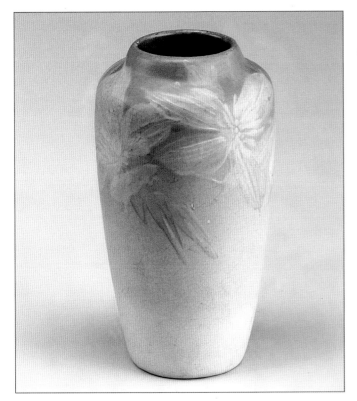

Early Hudson vase painted with pink clematis, identified with an impressed "WELLER" manufacturer's mark. 10" x 5". *Courtesy of David Rago Auctions.* $300-400.

Tall Hudson vase painted with dogwood flowers on a shaded ground, identified with an impressed "WELLER" manufacturer's mark. 10.5" x 4.75". *Courtesy of David Rago Auctions.* $300-400.

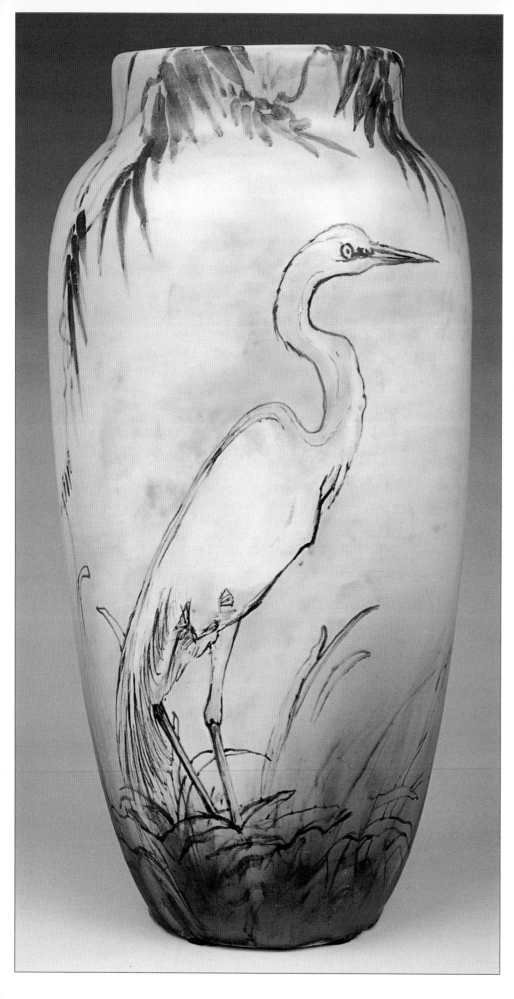

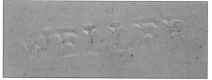

Unusual Hudson Scenic variant vase. The normal scenic vase has a drip overglaze, while this example is flat and white. It is identified with an impressed "WELLER" manufacturer's mark. 14" h. *Courtesy of Ken and Sharon Ballentine.* $5,500-6,000.

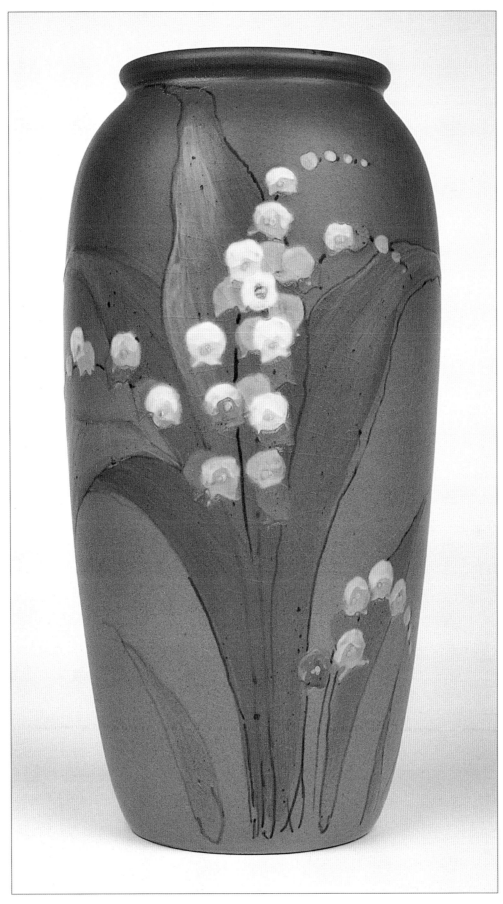

Hudson vase, "WELLER" impressed manufacturer's mark, 8.5" h.
Courtesy of Bob Shores and Dale Jones. $1,600-1,760.

Hudson vase, "WELLER" impressed manufacturer's mark, 8.25" h. *Courtesy of Bob Shores and Dale Jones.* $2,100-2,310.

Hudson classically-shaped vase painted with pink tulips, including a stamped WELLER mark. 11" x 4.25". *Courtesy of David Rago Auctions.* $600-900.

Hudson bulbous vase painted with wild roses and identified with a stamped mark. 8.75" x 3.75". *Courtesy of David Rago Auctions.* $350-450.

Hudson cylindrical vase painted with daffodils and identified with a stamped "WELLER" manufacturer's mark. 8.5" x 3.5". *Courtesy of David Rago Auctions.* $300-400.

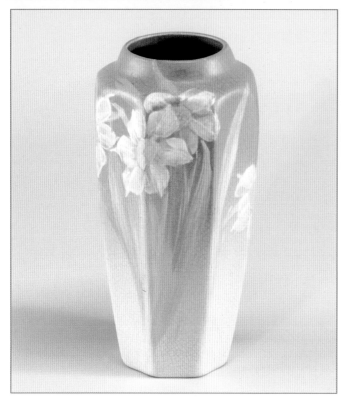

Hudson faceted vase painted with ivory and yellow jonquils, identified with a "WELLER" manufacturer's ink stamp mark. 9.75" x 4.75". *Courtesy of David Rago Auctions.* $300-400.

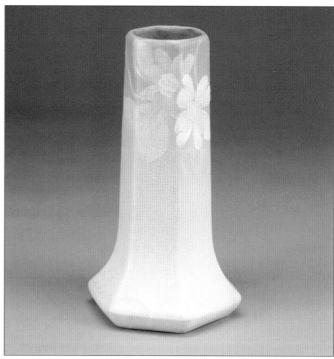

Hudson faceted vase painted with pink and white dogwood. 12" x 5.5". *Courtesy of David Rago Auctions.* $350-450.

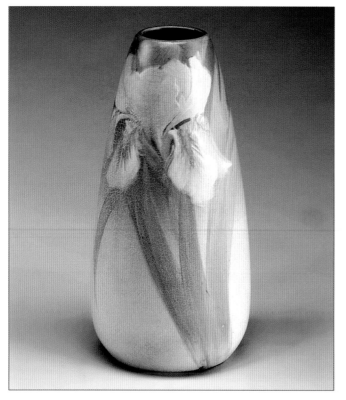

Hudson Light tear-shaped vase painted with iris, stamped "WELLER". 11" x 5.5". *Courtesy of David Rago Auctions.* $500-750.

Hudson Light pear-shaped vase painted with pink wild roses, identified with an impressed "WELLER" manufacturer's mark. 7.25" x 4.25". *Courtesy of David Rago Auctions.* $300-400.

Hudson Light vase with decoration of white and yellow roses. Marked "WELLER" in block letters. 3.5" h. *Courtesy of Mark Mussio, Cincinnati Art Galleries, LLC.* $150-250.

Blue and Decorated Hudson ovoid vase painted with a cluster of pink blossoms and band in pinks and greens, marked with a "WELLER" ink stamp. 8" x 5" *Courtesy of David Rago Auctions.* $200-300.

Blue and Decorated Hudson cylindrical vase painted with a cluster of pink blossoms, marked with an ink stamp. 7" x 3.25". *Courtesy of David Rago Auctions.* $100-200.

White and Decorated Hudson vase showing a profusion of maroon prunus blossoms with green leaves and black branches on an ivory ground. Impressed "WELLER" manufacturer's mark in large block letters. 9" h. *Courtesy of Mark Mussio, Cincinnati Art Galleries, LLC.* $250-350.

White and Decorated Hudson tapering vase painted with cherry blossoms, identified with an impressed "WELLER" manufacturer's mark. 7" x 4.25". *Courtesy of David Rago Auctions.* $200-300.

White and Decorated Hudson faceted vase painted with pink cherry blossoms, unmarked. 11.5" x 6". *Courtesy of David Rago Auctions.* $400-600.

Hunter squat vase, decorated by Edwin L. Pickens with two quizzical fish swimming around its perimeter. Incised "Hunter" on the bottom and signed "ELP" by the artist. 1.25" x 5". *Courtesy of Mark Mussio, Cincinnati Art Galleries, LLC.* $800-1,000.

Hunter vase with decoration of a bird flying above a large body of water, peering intently. Marked "Hunter X 862 7." 5.25" h. *Courtesy of Mark Mussio, Cincinnati Art Galleries, LLC.* $500-700.

Rare Hunter vase painted with seagulls flying over
the ocean, marked "R81X." 7.25" x 3". *Courtesy of
David Rago Auctions.* $450-650.

Hunter mug showing a
brown and white duck
floating on a lake.
Marked "Hunter 435
6." 6" h. *Courtesy of
Mark Mussio, Cincinnati
Art Galleries, LLC.*
$300-400.

Ivory: a.k.a. Clinton Ivory, c. 1928

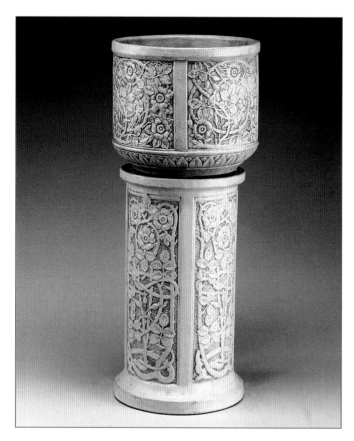

Ivory jardinière and pedestal embossed with rose vines, identified with an ink stamp manufacturer's mark. The jardinière measures 8.5" h.; the pedestal measures 16.25" h. *Courtesy of David Rago Auctions.* $350-500.

Jap Birdimal / Rhead Faience, 1904

Jap Birdimal ovoid vase with fish decoration in the squeeze bag technique, marked with the artist's initials "U.N.H." 6.25" x 3.25". *Courtesy of David Rago Auctions.* $750-1,000.

Jap Birdimal jardinière with landscape of indigo trees and full moon on a light blue ground, stamped "WELLER." 8.5" x 10.25". *Courtesy of David Rago Auctions.* $400-500.

Jap Birdimal two-handled mug painted with a Viking ship in dark blue on an ivory ground, identified with a "WELLER" stamp manufacturer's mark. 4" x 6.25". *Courtesy of David Rago Auctions.* $150-250.

Jap Birdimal creamer with Dutch landscape in shades of blue, identified with a raised Weller seal. 2.25" x 3.5". *Courtesy of David Rago Auctions.* $100-200.

Rhead Faience teapot decorated with Viking ships circumnavigating the pot's base with colorful, stylized decoration shown above. Marked "F 1 4 X." The lid is missing and the handle is cracked. 11.5" h. *Courtesy of Mark Mussio, Cincinnati Art Galleries, LLC.* $400-500.

Juneau, c. 1930s

Juneau vase, dating from the early 1930s, glazed in shades of pinkish reds with highlights of ivory, blue, and green. The vase is identified with an ink stamped "Weller Pottery" manufacturer's mark. 10.25" h. *Courtesy of Mark Mussio, Cincinnati Art Galleries, LLC.* $200-300.

Kenova, middle period (1918-1935)

Possibly unique Kenova vase featuring a red rose on a possibly experimental mat green background. Marked "WELLER" in block letters. A "White Pillars Museum" label is affixed to the base. 8" h. *Courtesy of Mark Mussio, Cincinnati Art Galleries, LLC.* $1,200-1,500.

Knifewood, 1915-1920

Knifewood vessel decorated with swans gliding across still water in a forest setting, identified with an impressed WELLER manufacturer's mark. 5" x 3". *Courtesy of David Rago Auctions.* $300-400.

Klyro Ware, middle period (1918-1935)

Klyro chamber stick with branches of cherries, unmarked. 5.75" d. *Courtesy of David Rago Auctions.* $150-250.

Lamar scenic vase decorated with pine trees and a mountain under red luster glaze. Unmarked. There are some minor glaze rubs, often seen with this line. 8" h. *Courtesy of Mark Mussio, Cincinnati Art Galleries, LLC.* $200-300.

Unusual and large LaSa baluster vase painted with green trees in front of a purple lake, green hills, and yellow sky, identified with a "Weller LaSa" mark on the body. 13.5" x 6.5". *Courtesy of David Rago Auctions.* $400-600.

Both sides of the large LaSa vase with two different hand-painted trees and landscapes. Unmarked. 13.5" h. *Courtesy of Arnie Small and Barbara Gerr.* $400-600.

A pair of LaSa bud vases, unmarked. 7.25" h. each.
Courtesy of David Rago Auctions. $400-500.

LaSa ovoid vase painted
with palm trees on a
golden horizon,
unmarked. 6.5" x 3.5".
*Courtesy of David Rago
Auctions.* $250-350.

LaSa bowl with landscape in shades of pink and gold, unmarked.
9" d. *Courtesy of David Rago Auctions.* $300-400.

Lorbeek four piece console set consisting of a 3" x 13.75" bowl, a 5" flower holder, and two 2.5" candle holders, all in an Art Deco style of stepped geometric form and covered with a lavender semi-gloss glaze. Marked with a "Weller Ware" blue ink stamp manufacturer's mark. Cincinnati Art Galleries states, "Lorbeek was Weller's deepest bow to the Deco movement." *Courtesy of Mark Mussio, Cincinnati Art Galleries, LLC.* $200-300.

Louella, c. 1915-1920

Louella vase with painted
flowers, vertical ribbing,
grayish body mat glaze, c.
1915. 23" h. *Courtesy of Bob
Shores and Dale Jones.* $950.

Louwelsa ovoid vase painted with nasturtiums, possibly by Ruth Axline, identified with an impressed manufacturer's mark and an artist's cipher. 8.25" x 3.5". *Courtesy of David Rago Auctions.* $200-300.

Louwelsa ovoid vase finely painted by Levi Burgess with roses, identified with both a stamped manufacturer's mark and the artist's cipher. 14.75" x 5". *Courtesy of David Rago Auctions.* $200-300.

Large Louwelsa bulbous vase painted by Frank Ferrell with a branch of grapes, marked "432/Ferrell". 12" x 8". *Courtesy of David Rago Auctions.* $600-900.

Louwelsa mug decorated and signed by Frank Ferrell with purple grapes on a vine. Marks include the "Weller Louwelsa" mark, impressed "562 2," incised "L," and slip painted decorator's mark on the mug's surface. 5.75" h. *Courtesy of Mark Mussio, Cincinnati Art Galleries, LLC.* $150-200.

Louwelsa tall two-handled vase painted by W. Hall with nasturtiums, identified with a stamped maker's mark and the artist's cipher. 15" x 5.25". *Courtesy of David Rago Auctions.* $450-650.

Louwelsa two-handled, tear-shaped vase with yellow daffodils by Minnie Mitchell, marked "LOUWELSA WELLER/M. Mitchell." 10" h. *Courtesy of David Rago Auctions.* $250-350.

Louwelsa jug by Minnie Mitchell, painted with cherries, identified with an impressed manufacturer's mark and the artist's initials. 6" h. *Courtesy of David Rago Auctions.* $150-250.

Louwelsa vase with yellow daffodils painted by Amelia Brown Sprague. The base is impressed with a semi-circular "Weller Louwelsa" maker's mark and the numbers "151 3," while the artist's initials are in brown slip near the decoration. 13.5" h. *Courtesy of Mark Mussio, Cincinnati Art Galleries, LLC.* $300-400.

Louwelsa squat vessel painted by "A. S." (Amelia Brown Sprague?) with branches of wild roses, impressed mark. 3" x 5.5". *Courtesy of David Rago Auctions.* $300-400.

Louwelsa ewer painted with a yellow rose, identified with an impressed "LOUWELSA WELLER" mark and artist's initials "M.I." 7" x 6". *Courtesy of David Rago Auctions.* $100-200.

Louwelsa pitcher adorned with wild roses by an unknown artist. Marked "Louwelsa Weller 508 4." 5" h. *Courtesy of Mark Mussio, Cincinnati Art Galleries, LLC.* $100-150.

Louwelsa lamp vase with a Tiffany-style Swirling Leaf leaded glass shade and Tiffany font. The base is decorated with nasturtiums and artist signed (initials illegible). It is impressed with a "Louwelsa Weller" mark inside. 11" h. ceramic base; 20.25" h. overall. The original oil fittings were replaced with electrical fittings. *Courtesy of Mark Mussio, Cincinnati Art Galleries, LLC.* $2,500-3,500.

Louwelsa three-handled pillow vase, impressed manufacturer's mark on the base. 6.5" h. *Courtesy of Ken and Sharon Ballentine.* $325-375.

Louwelsa pillow vase painted with orange and white carnations, identified with a stamped manufacturer's mark. 4". *Courtesy of David Rago Auctions.* $125+.

Louwelsa pillow vase painted with wild rose, identified with an impressed "LOUWELSA WELLER/8/X" mark. 4" x 5.25". *Courtesy of David Rago Auctions.* $150-250.

Louwelsa squat ewer painted with a rose, impressed manufacturer's mark. 4.25" x 5.5". *Courtesy of David Rago Auctions.* $150-250.

Louwelsa squat jug painted with oak branches, stamped "WELLER LOUWELSA". 3.25" x 5.75". *Courtesy of David Rago Auctions.* $100-200.

Louwelsa oil lamp base painted with nasturtiums, identified with a stamped maker's mark. 17" h. *Courtesy of David Rago Auctions.* $500-700.

Blue Louwelsa cylindrical vase decorated with two pansy blooms on a rich blue background, identified with an impressed "WELLER" manufacturer's mark in block letters. 5" h. *Courtesy of Mark Mussio, Cincinnati Art Galleries, LLC.* $400-600.

Blue Louwelsa vase lavishly decorated with poppies and buds. Marked with the circular "Louwelsa Weller" impressed stamp. 11.5" h. *Courtesy of Mark Mussio, Cincinnati Art Galleries, LLC.* $700-900.

Lustre: a.k.a. Luster, 1920

Two Lustre vases, unmarked. 6" and 8" h. *Courtesy of David Rago Auctions.* $100-200 each.

Malvern, middle period (1918-1935)

Malvern pillow vase identified with a script
"Weller" manufacturer's mark. 8" x 6.5".
Courtesy of David Rago Auctions. $200-300.

Malvern ovoid vase,
marked. 6.5" h.
*Courtesy of David Rago
Auctions.* $150-250.

Manhattan, late period (1935-1948)

Green Manhattan flaring vase
marked "Weller Pottery" in script.
9" x 5". *Courtesy of David Rago
Auctions.* $75-125.

Marvo, c. 1928

Green Marvo umbrella stand identified with an ink stamp and paper label. 19.5" x 11". *Courtesy of David Rago Auctions.* $300-500.

Brown Marvo jardinière and pedestal, identified with an ink kiln stamp. The pedestal measures 22.25" h.; the jardinière measures 10.5" h. *Courtesy of David Rago Auctions.* $400-500.

Matt Green, middle period (1918-1935)

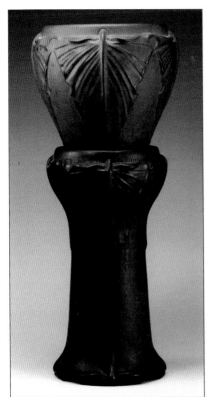

Matt Green jardinière and pedestal embossed with broad leaves, unmarked Jardinière: 11.5" x 13". *Courtesy of David Rago Auctions.* $500-600.

Matt Green jardinière embossed with broad leaves under a smooth glaze, unmarked. 8.5" x 11". *Courtesy of David Rago Auctions.* $300-400.

Matt Green vase with embossed,
stylized flowers. Impressed "Weller"
in large block letters. 10.25" h.
*Courtesy of Mark Mussio, Cincinnati
Art Galleries, LLC.* $250-350.

Tall Matt Green corseted vase impressed with
geometric designs, unmarked. 15.25" x 7".
Courtesy of David Rago Auctions. $500-700.

Matt Green jardinière embossed with broad leaves, identified with a stamped "WELLER" manufacturer's mark. 11" x 12.25". *Courtesy of David Rago Auctions.* $400-600.

Matt Green jardinière with four buttressed handles, unmarked. 6.75" x 9". *Courtesy of David Rago Auctions.* $200-300.

Matt Green jardinière embossed with Greek key pattern and buttresses, unmarked. 8.25" x 10.5". *Courtesy of David Rago Auctions.* $350-450.

Matt Green corseted vase with incised geometric designs, unmarked. 15.5". *Courtesy of David Rago Auctions.* $500-700.

Matt Green vase with incised detail and four vertical buttresses, unmarked. 9.5" h. *Courtesy of Arnie Small and Barbara Gerr.* $250-350.

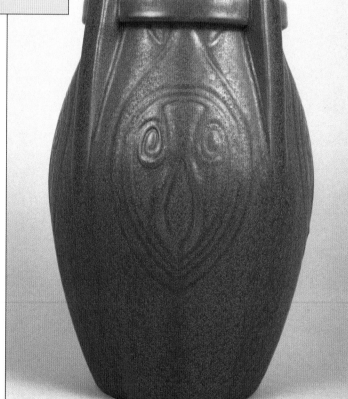

Rare Muskota fish bowl holder with playful cat figurine and trunk-shaped bud vase, identified with a "WELLER" stamp manufacturer's mark. 11" x 11.25". *Courtesy of David Rago Auctions.* $1,500-2,000.

Muskota fish bowl holder with a Kingfisher perched on a tree stump staring intently into the bowl. Impressed "WELLER" manufacturer's mark in block letters. 13.5" x 11". *Courtesy of Mark Mussio, Cincinnati Art Galleries, LLC.* $400-500.

Muskota figure of a woman kneeling in the rushes, her back hand has a
hole to hold a slender object, impressed "WELLER" manufacturer's
mark. 6" h. *Courtesy of Arnie Small and Barbara Gerr.* $360-400.

Muskota white duck figural, unmarked. 5.25" l.
Courtesy of Arnie Small and Barbara Gerr. $300-330.

Swan and Muskota figure of a girl with a watering can flower frogs, swan with impressed
"WELLER" manufacturer's mark, the Muskota girl figure is unmarked. Girl: 6.5" h.
Courtesy of Arnie Small and Barbara Gerr. Swan: $390-430; girl: $550-600.

Muskota nude child
kneeling flower frog,
unmarked. 4" h.
*Courtesy of Arnie Small
and Barbara Gerr.*
$550-600.

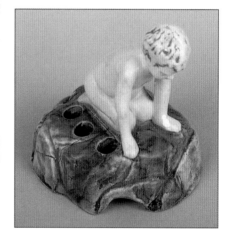

Muskota flower frog with
two swimming trout by a
log, covered in a glossy
green glaze, stamped
"WELLER." 5" x 4".
*Courtesy of David Rago
Auctions.* $600+.

Muskota flower-frog with the frog on a white water lily, stamped "WELLER" manufacturer's mark. 5" x 4.75". *Courtesy of David Rago Auctions.* $330+.

Muskota geese planter with three geese figures in white along one side, impressed "WELLER" manufacturer's mark. 7.25" h. *Courtesy of Arnie Small and Barbara Gerr.* $520-570.

Muskota flower frog with a turtle bearing a lily pad on his back, marked "WELLER" in impressed block letters. 4.25" x 9.5". *Courtesy of Mark Mussio, Cincinnati Art Galleries, LLC.* $440+.

Neiska, 1933-1936

Neiska blue bulbous vase with twisted handles, indentified on the base with an incised manufacturer's mark. *Courtesy of David Rago Auctions.* $240-360.

Paragon, late period (1935-1948)

Paragon vase, dating from circa 1935, molded decoration of flowers and leaves covered with a dark red mat glaze. Identified with a "Weller" script manufacturer's mark. 4.5" h. *Courtesy of Mark Mussio, Cincinnati Art Galleries, LLC.* $70-100.

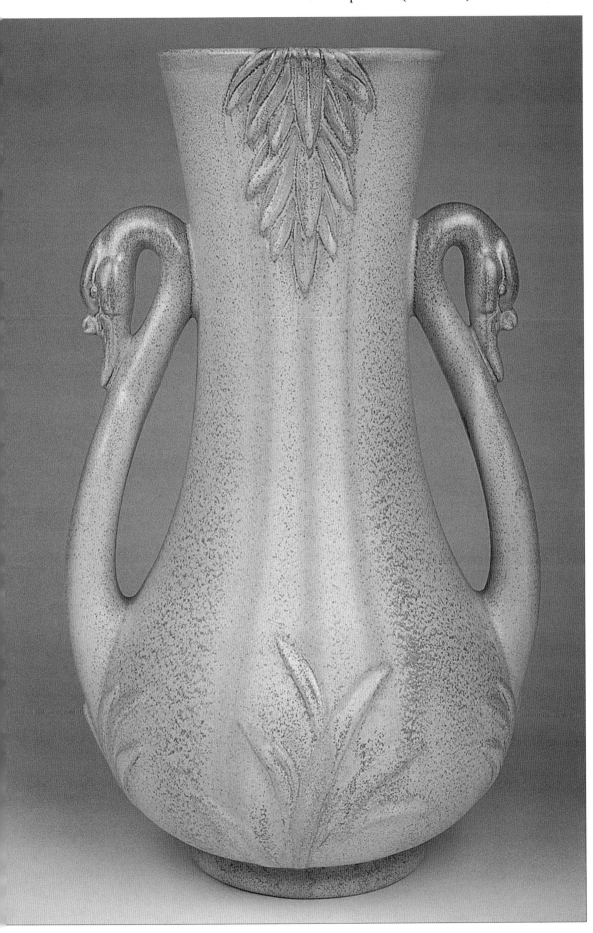

Patricia vase with
swan handles. 18" h.
*Courtesy of Ken and
Sharon Ballentine.*
$600-800.

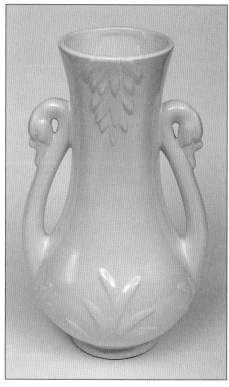

White Patricia vase. 18" h. *Courtesy of Ken and Sharon Ballentine.* $500-700.

Patricia handled pot, "Weller" impressed manufacturer's mark. 6" h. *Courtesy of Ken and Sharon Ballentine.* $150-175.

Patricia vase in semi-gloss white glaze, graceful swan necks and heads serve as handles with stylized leaves decorating the body. Unmarked. 17.5". *Courtesy of Mark Mussio, Cincinnati Art Galleries, LLC.* $500-700.

Pearl, 1915-1920

Back: Pearl jardinière. 5" h.
Front: Tivoli comport. 6" h.
These items are found marked with a stamped "Weller" maker's mark. *Courtesy of David Rago Auctions.* $100-200 each.

Perfecto, early period (1895-1918)
Painted decoration over unglazed ceramics.

Perfecto tankard signed by Frank Ferrell. 12" h.
Courtesy of Ken and Sharon Ballentine. $3,000-3,500.

Roma, c. 1919

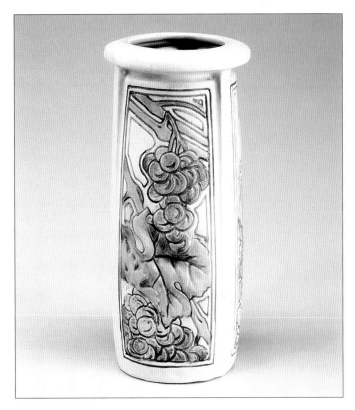

Roma buttressed vase decorated with grapes, unmarked.
10" x 4.5". *Courtesy of David Rago Auctions.* $150-250.

Roma wall pocket with swags of red roses,
stamped "WELLER" manufacturer's mark. 7.25".
Courtesy of David Rago Auctions. $50-100.

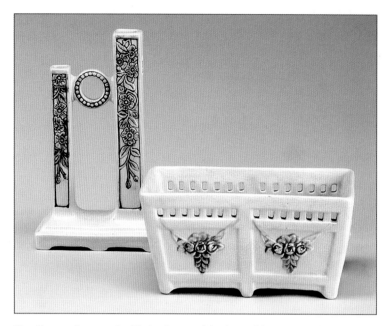

Two Roma pieces: a double bud vase with cherry blossoms and a
rectangular planter with roses. The vase measures 6.5" h. *Courtesy
of David Rago Auctions.* $200-300.

Unusual Roma doorstop in the form of a basket of fruit, impressed
"Weller" manufacturer's mark in large block letters. 9.25" h.
Courtesy of Mark Mussio, Cincinnati Art Galleries, LLC. $400-600.

Rosemont vase with two molded blue jays on flowering tree branches (one on each side) against a glossy black glaze, impressed "WELLER" manufacturer's mark. 9.75" h. *Courtesy of Bob Shores and Dale Jones.* $565-625.

Sicard pillow vase with scalloped rim and handles painted with golden and green blossoms on a red luster ground, stamped "WELLER/34". 6.25" x 9.75". *Courtesy of David Rago Auctions.* $1,500-2,000.

Sicard vase with two short handles with clover leaves and dots across the entire surface, marks include the "Sicard" signature on the side and the number "38" and the letter "W" on the base. 4.5" h. *Courtesy of Mark Mussio, Cincinnati Art Galleries, LLC.* $1,000-1,500.

Sicard vase with decoration of spider mums in iridescent colors of gold, green, red, and blue, signed "Weller" and "Sicard" on the side. 9.75" h. *Courtesy of Mark Mussio, Cincinnati Art Galleries, LLC.* $1,200-1,700.

Sicard pillow vase decorated with spider mums under a nacreous green, red, and orange glaze, marked "WELLER Sicard" in script. 10.5" x 6". *Courtesy of David Rago Auctions.* $1,000-1,200.

Sicard gourd-shaped vase with peacock feathers in red,
green, and blue, marked "Weller Sicard" in script. 5.5"
x 5". *Courtesy of David Rago Auctions.* $800-1,000.

Sicard tapering vase with falling leaves and wavy lines under
nacreous purple, green, and yellow glaze, marked "WELLER
SICARD". 5" x 3.5". *Courtesy of David Rago Auctions.* $700-950.

Sicard vase decorated with stylized chrysanthemums on a
nacreous blue, purple, red, and gold ground, signed "Weller
Sicardo." 9" x 5". *Courtesy of David Rago Auctions.* $750-1,000.

Sicard tapering vase with flat shoulder, small flowers amidst tall
blades of grass, covered in a nacreous green glaze, marked "Weller
Sicard". 4" x 4". *Courtesy of David Rago Auctions.* $600-900.

Sicard circular bowl with four buttresses and decorated with clover under
a nacreous red, purple, and green glaze, marked "Weller." 2.5" x 6.5".
Courtesy of David Rago Auctions. $550-750.

Sicard bud vase with triangular opening, painted with
stars and moons in red, blue, and gold lustered glaze,
identified with a "Weller Sicard" script mark. 4.5" x 2.75".
Courtesy of David Rago Auctions. $500-750.

Sicard bulbous tapering vase with flowers and dots under a nacreous purple, blue, green, and gold glaze, marked "Weller Sicard." 3.75" x 3". *Courtesy of David Rago Auctions.* $500-750.

Sicard four-sided cabinet vase with daisies, signed "Sicard Weller" in script. 4.5" x 2.5". *Courtesy of David Rago Auctions.* $450-650.

Sicard candlestick with stars and butterflies in green and burgundy luster glaze, signed "Weller Sicard". 6.5". *Courtesy of David Rago Auctions.* $450-650.

Sicard cabinet vase decorated with falling leaves, signed "Sicard Weller" in script. 4.5" x 3". *Courtesy of David Rago Auctions.* $400-600.

Sicard bulbous bud vase with mistletoe in green and purple luster glazes, signed "WELLER." 4.75" x 2.5". *Courtesy of David Rago Auctions.* $300-400.

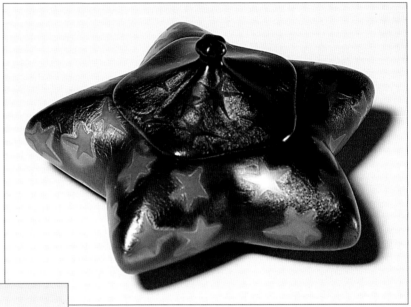

Sicard star-shaped covered box, decorated with stars spangling the surface of the box and lid, unmarked. 2.5". *Courtesy of Mark Mussio, Cincinnati Art Galleries, LLC.* $300-400.

Sicard bud vase decorated with flowers on a nacreous gold, green, and purple ground, signed "Weller Sicard." 5.25" x 2.5". *Courtesy of David Rago Auctions.* $250-350.

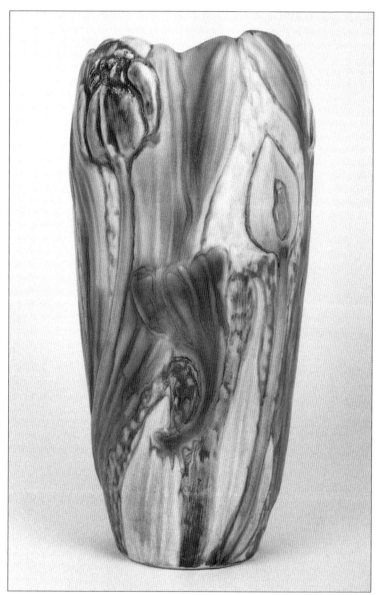

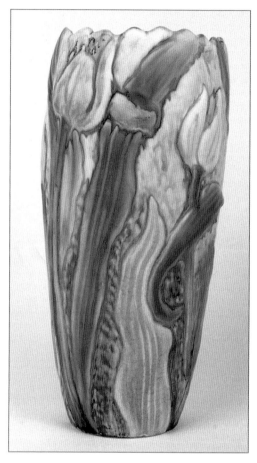

Silvertone tulip vase with embossed tulips glazed for color, marked "Weller Ware" with a printed manufacturer's mark. 9.75" h. *Courtesy of Arnie Small and Barbara Gerr.* $800-880.

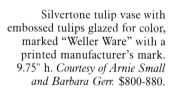

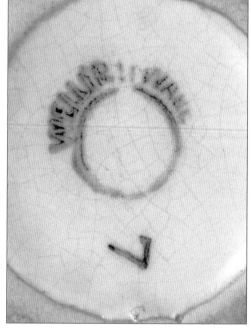

Rare Silvertone fan vase embossed with dogwood blossoms, covered in a Coppertone variation glaze, unmarked. 8" x 10.5".
Courtesy of David Rago Auctions. $400-500.

Stellar, 1934
Stellar was glazed in either a black or blue ground with white stars.

Stellar blue ground glaze bulbous vase by Hester Pillsbury, identified with the script "Weller Pottery" manufacturer's mark and the artist's initials. 6" x 6.5".
Courtesy of David Rago Auctions. $770-1,100.

Tivoli, 1915-1920
See Pearl for an example of a Tivoli comport.

Tupelo, middle period (1918-1935)

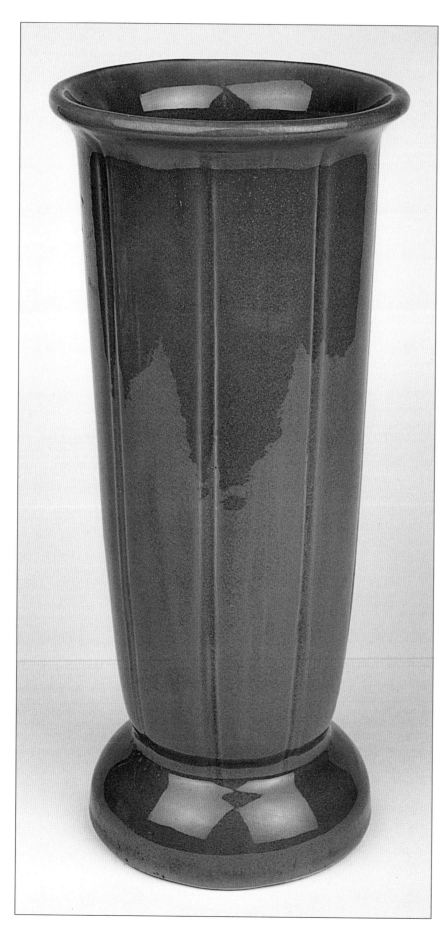

Tupelo vase. Green glaze, vertical ribbing (single lines), impressed "Weller Pottery" script manufacturer's mark. 13.75" h. *Courtesy of Bob Shores and Dale Jones.* $225-250.

Turada, 1897-1898

Turada corseted planter, unmarked. 7.75" x 8.25".
Courtesy of David Rago Auctions. $200-300.

Turada corseted bowl, identified with a stamped
"Turada" manufacturer's mark. 3.25" x 8" d.
Courtesy of David Rago Auctions. $100-200.

Tutone, middle period (1918-1935)

Tutone three-sided vase with
panels of green blossoms and
leaves on a pink ground, unmarked. 9" x 5.5". *Courtesy of
David Rago Auctions.* $400-500.

Velva vase with two handles, green with embossed and glazed decoration. 8.5" h. *Courtesy of Arnie Small and Barbara Gerr.* $110-220.

Velva two-handled vase glazed in blue with embossed and glazed decoration, identified on the base with a script "Weller" manufacturer's mark. 8.5" h. *Courtesy of David Rago Auctions.* $110-220.

Velvetone, 1928

Velvetone matt green vase with raised stylized designs covered in vellum glaze, identified as "Velvetone Ware" on a paper label. 6" x 5.75". *Courtesy of David Rago Auctions.* $350-450.

Voile, middle period (1918-1935)

Voile fan vase produced during the 1920s, marked. 5.5" h. *Courtesy of David Rago Auctions.* $150-250.

Warwick, middle period (1918-1935)

Warwick cylindrical vase. 9" h. *Courtesy of David Rago Auctions.* $100-200.

Wild Rose, 1930-1936

Wild Rose two-handled vase and pitcher, each glazed in matte orange transitioning to green, each identified on the base with a script "Weller" manufacturer's mark. Vase: 13" h. Pitcher: 12" h. *Courtesy of David Rago Auctions.* $180-300 each.

Woodcraft, c. 1917-1928

A pair of Woodcraft cylindrical vases decorated with branches and pink blossoms, unmarked. 10.25" each. *Courtesy of David Rago Auctions.* $200-300 each.

Two examples of the Woodcraft double bud vase with apples on branches decoration, unmarked. 7.5" x 8". Note the variations in the glazes. *Courtesy of David Rago Auctions.* $150-250 each.

Woodcraft bud vase, unmarked. 8.75" x 3.25".
Courtesy of David Rago Auctions. $150-200.

Woodcraft jardinière with woodpecker, identified with an impressed "WELLER" manufacturer's mark. 6.5" x 8.5". *Courtesy of David Rago Auctions.* $450-650.

Woodcraft jardinière with woodpecker, unmarked. 6.5"h. x 6.5" d. *Courtesy of Arnie Small and Barbara Gerr.* $400-440.

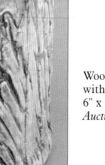

Woodcraft "Little Foxes" planter with foxes in their den, unmarked. 6" x 7". *Courtesy of David Rago Auctions.* $300-400.

Woodcraft "Little Foxes" bowl glazed in lifelike colors, marked only with an ink stamped "B." 4.25" x 7.5". *Courtesy of Mark Mussio, Cincinnati Art Galleries, LLC.* $300-400.

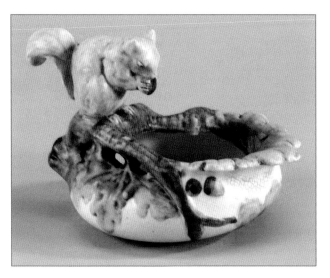

Woodcraft dish with figure of squirrel perched on rim, identified with a kiln stamp manufacturer's mark. 5" x 6.5". *Courtesy of David Rago Auctions.* $100-200.

Woodcraft bowl with squirrels in the forest, unmarked. 7" d. *Courtesy of David Rago Auctions.* $200-300.

Woodcraft bird dogs figural piece, marked with an impressed "WELLER" manufacturer's mark. 12" h x 7" l. *Courtesy of Arnie Small and Barbara Gerr.* $1,200+.

Woodcraft wall plaque with birds in branches, unmarked. Small holes at the ends of the branches (top ends). 15.5" long. *Courtesy of Arnie Small and Barbara Gerr.* $1,140-1,440.

Wood Rose: a.k.a. Woodrose, 1915-1920

Wood Rose baskets and a vase, each identified with an impressed "WELLER" manufacturer's mark. Vase: 10" h. *Courtesy of David Rago Auctions.* $240-360 each.

Xenia

Xenia vase, gray with red flowers in Art Nouveau style, impressed Weller manufacturer's mark. 11" high. *Courtesy of Arnie Small and Barbara Gerr.* $2,655-2,920.

Zona, c. 1920

The early design, by Rudolph Lorber, featured red apples on branches (the design that would become Gladding, McBean & Company's Apple line). Afterwards, the Zona line featured baskets, jars, and pitchers adorned with cattails and kingfishers in relief designs and the Zona Baby line. The Zona Baby line is comprised of a children's bowl, plate, cup, and pitcher ornamented with cute squirrels, a duck, bunny, bird, or Mary and her famous lamb. The Zona Baby line was in production for roughly a decade from c. 1926-1936.

Two Zona 9.75" serving plates, each identified with an ink stamp manufacturer's mark. *Courtesy of David Rago Auctions.* $100-200 each.

Zona Kingfisher pitcher with panels of cattails and kingfisher, identified with a kiln stamp manufacturer's mark. 8" x 8.5". *Courtesy of David Rago Auctions.* $515-575.

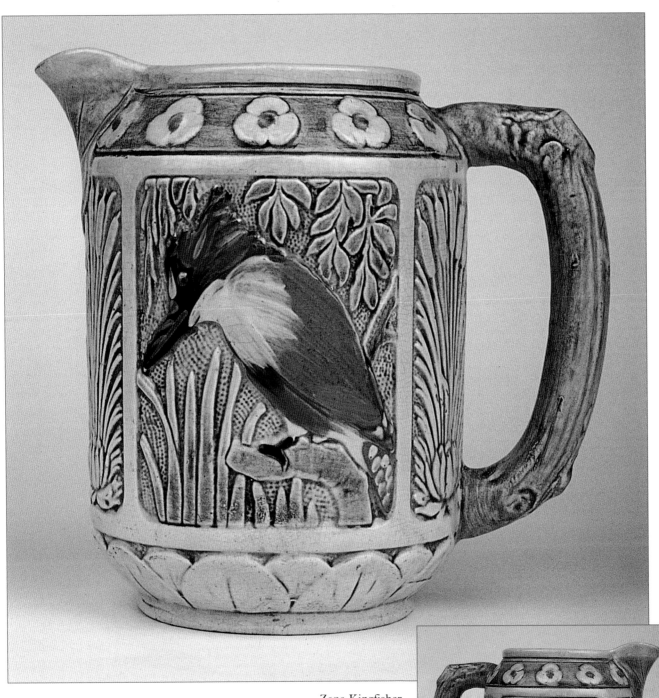

Zona Kingfisher pitcher with a tree on the back side and cattails in front. 8" h. to rim. *Courtesy of Bob Shores and Dale Jones.* $515-575.

Parting Words

Just a few words on collecting, quality, fakery, and meaning before we part. Weller pottery attracts a large, enthusiastic, and ever-growing number of collectors today. The beauty of the ware and the vast range of products are appealing factors for many. When just starting out, the first thing one needs for successful collecting is information. If you wish to find additional information on Weller ceramics, knowledgeable dealers, auction catalogs, and collector's organizations (try the American Art Pottery Association) are invaluable resources well worth tapping. However, now that you have gathered some information and feel comfortable with the subject ... and the prices ... you should feel confident enough to begin collecting Weller pottery.

When collecting, the initial urge is to snap up every piece you find. Resist temptation! Collect the things you love and buy the best quality items that you can afford. That may mean limiting yourself to a collection of modest size. However, by collecting the best within your range, you will end up with a far better collection. Buying the best means knowing what to look for and avoiding damaged goods. Also, keep alert, as you never know where the next find will come from. Prowl the antique malls and fairs, general auctions, moving sales, garage sales, and flea markets. While learning to identify the many Weller pottery lines, the most reliable guarantee that you have ceramics produced by the correct company comes in the form of the aforementioned manufacturer's marks. Begin by collecting marked pieces for peace of mind.

Some find it useful to collect one particular line or to collect thematically. This narrows the vast range of Weller products to more manageable proportions. With the many different decorative motifs and figural wares Weller produced, the company's wares are well suited for any number of innovative collecting themes.

In an article for *Better Homes & Gardens* magazine in 1936, author Vivan Davis provided some useful suggestions to help determine the quality of a piece of pottery. Davis wrote, "No one but a ceramics expert can walk into a shop where a variety of pottery is displayed and merely by glancing at it tell which is good and which is inferior. There are, however, a number of tests that will help us determine the worth and durability of the ware." (Davis 1936, 83) Three factors were listed that help determine the quality of the ware being examined: weight, glaze, and finish. First Davis suggested that, unless dealing with ovenware, if a piece feels unusually heavy for its size then it is probably made of inferior materials and will not wear well over time. In glazing, Davis recommended examining the glaze carefully. If the glaze is darker in some areas than others, it was not fired properly, will not resist heat or cold well, and will eventually begin to chip or craze. Also, she suggested looking for air holes in the glaze; these tiny pinpricks in the surface weaken the finish. As for finish, Davis recommended checking the small stilt marks (an artifact of pottery production to be discussed below) on the base of the pottery. If the stilt marks are rough to the touch, the pottery company responsible is careless and does not either finish or inspect their products well. Smooth stilt marks were considered to be an indication of higher quality control within the factory and a sign of a better overall product.

Effects of Pottery Production

It is worth taking a moment to discuss some of the more common factory flaws that may be found on pottery. While these factory flaws will lower the value of the ceramics they are found on, they should not be mistakenly identified as indications that the pottery has been damaged at some time after it was produced.

When glaze has been applied to the body of any vessel, some method must be used to keep the glaze from hardening to the sagger (a protective clay box into which pottery is placed prior to its insertion into the kiln) during firing. Two common methods used to keep the glaze out of contact with the sagger are the dry foot and the stilt. The foot is the base upon which a ceramic object rests. Using the dry foot method, by carefully removing any traces of glaze from the foot prior to firing—ensuring that the foot is "dry," the potter ensures that glaze will not come into contact with the sagger and that the pottery will not adhere it.

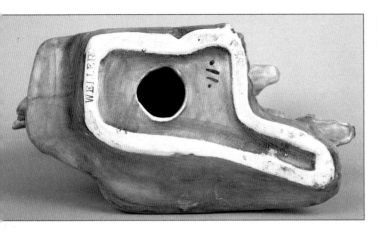

Here is a fine example of the dry foot. Using the dry foot method, by carefully removing any traces of glaze from the foot prior to firing—ensuring that the foot is "dry," the potter ensures that glaze will not come into contact with the sagger and that the pottery will not adhere it. *Courtesy of Arnie Small and Barbara Gerr.*

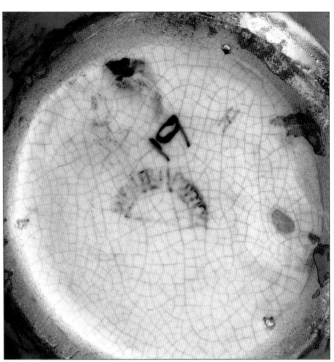

Note the three stilt marks just inside the foot rim. The stilt kept the glazed base of this Coppertone vase from sticking to the fire sagger. *Courtesy of Arnie Small and Barbara Gerr.*

If it is desirable for the bottom of a piece to be glazed, then the glazed surface may be kept out of contact with the surrounding sagger by using stilts. A stilt is a small, Y-shaped bisque support, a type of "kiln furniture," with projections reaching up above and down below the Y. A pot with a glaze-coated base may be placed on the stilt's projecting, ends within the sagger, keeping the glazed base raised up off the bottom of the sagger. During firing, as the glaze hardens, it adheres to the stilt at those three small points. Once the firing was complete, and the kiln cooled, it was a simple matter to give the pot a quick twist to snap it free from the stilt. Left behind on the base of the pot are three glaze free tell-tale dots where the stilt supported the piece. These are called "stilt marks" and should not be mistaken for damage.

Pottery production does not always go smoothly. Mistakes are made and some pottery is produced with imperfections. Depending on the standards of the potting firms involved, wares featuring small irregularities may have been overlooked entirely or they may have been sold as factory seconds. Pieces with manufacturing flaws will be valued lower in the collectibles market than their pristine brethren but such pieces once again should not be considered damaged goods.

Common factory flaws include unusual glaze color variations, visible mold seam lines, uneven bases, ill-fitting lids, and handles that do not match in proportion or placement. Glaze crazing is a common flaw. Crazing occurs when the clay body and glaze cool at different rates, creating thin cracks in the glaze. This event would not occur among the late Weller products. Such items had the body and glaze fired together, rather than the clay body fired hard first, then glazed and fired a second time. In the single firing process of Weller's later years, the glaze actually fuses into the ceramic body, eliminating crazing.

At times, pottery chipped in the bisque stage was glazed and fired anyway. On close inspection you will note in this case that the glaze completely covers the break. Along this line, at times pots have been glazed and fired with tiny crumbs of clay sticking to an otherwise smooth surface. These clay bits should have been removed prior to glazing and firing, but were missed by the potter. Finally, "kiln kisses" occur when a pot touches either the sagger wall or another pot as it is being loaded into the sagger for firing, leaving dents or unglazed areas on the pot.

Fakery

"You get what you pay for" is a truism that applies to Weller ceramics. Any collector should be wary of that really great deal. Pieces sold very inexpensively may be damaged in some way or they might be forgeries. Unfortunately, as Weller ceramics have become both increasingly popular and more expensive, Weller forgeries have become profitable. The simplest way to spot a forgery is by size. Forgeries tend to be smaller than their real counterparts by roughly ten percent. The reason for the size discrepancy is that forgers tend to use actual pottery to create their molds. Since ceramics shrink in the kiln, pottery produced from such a mold will be smaller than the original sculptural work from which the real mold was made by the pottery company. Of course, not having an original to compare with a suspicious piece, and knowing that some pieces were made in several sizes, complicates matters.

When you suspect something is wrong, look closely at the sharpness of the mold design. Details on forgeries tend to be less sharp than originals, although originals produced from a mold that is nearing the end of its useful life will also have less pronounced features. If size and sharpness are not conclusive, weight can help differentiate the real from the fraudulent. Original Weller pieces should be heavier than cheap imitations.

Take a close look at the color of the body clay as well. Clay from Zanesville, Ohio, fires to a buff color. With rare exceptions, different color will be indicative of a pretender produced elsewhere. Also, with Weller pottery you will generally find *some* unglazed surface underneath the piece where the manufacturer's mark is found. This is both convenient for checking body color and as a tip-off to a fake. A fake Weller item may well have an entirely glazed base.

Finally, keep your eyes open for suspicious abundance. If an item you know is rare starts to show up in large numbers, that is a good warning sign that forgeries are afoot.

A Matter of Meaning

The meaning Weller pottery had for the original purchasers was explored earlier. Collectors today find the assemblages they amass meaningful as well. Collectors can all tell tales of acquisition about various pieces. In the same way the objects in the Irish cupboard were filled with memories and associations, pieces in a modern collection trigger memories of acquisition, tales of "the hunt." It does not end there, either. Frequently, the collected items are fondly associated with other collectors met (and occasionally thwarted at auction), lasting friendships forged, and with stories of adventures far from home.

The arrangement of these artifacts on display often holds meaning as well. Items closely associated with each other may represent discoveries made by the collector, significance not readily ascertained by the casual viewer. As in Victorian society, collections often act as a buffer against the frequently harsh outside world. The Arts and Crafts Movement proponents hoped wares depicting nature would soothe the nerves at the end of the day in the busy, modern world. In simialar fashion, Weller collections frequently have that effect on those who gather them.

In all these ways, each collection of Weller amassed will be unique, each reflecting the personality of its owner. Each represents a personal journey of discovery and accumulated years spent on the quest. At times, collectors express regret that friends or family do not share their enthusiasm for their collections. But really, what makes any collection special is the meaning it holds for the collector. Collecting is a very personal experience.

Here's to the adventure and years of happy discovery ahead.

Opposite page:
The Arts and Crafts Movement proponents hoped wares depicting nature would soothe the nerves at the end of the day in the busy, modern world. Weller collections frequently have that effect on those who gather them. Hudson Floral vase by Sarah McLaughlin, signed by the artist near the base, "Weller Pottery" incised script manufacturer's mark. 15" h. *Courtesy of Ken and Sharon Ballentine.* $3,800-4,200.

Bibliography

"2003 Exhibition Schedule." Mulvane Art Museum Upcoming Events. <http:// www.washburn.edu/reference/Mulvane/upcomingevents.html>

"About Weller Pottery." Just Art Pottery. 2003. <http:// www.justartpottery.com/ collectors_pottery/ weller_pottery_history.html>

Albertson, Karla Klein. "How a Philadelphian gave American pottery a push." *The Philadelphia Inquirer*, November 14, 2003.

"Art Nouveau Glass and Pottery: Selections from the Syracuse University Art." November 10, 2002-January 26, 2003. Lora Robins Gallery of Design from Nature, University of Richmond Museums.

"The Arts and Crafts Movement in Victoria, British Columbia." <http://www. maltwood.uvic.ca/ ~maltwood/arts-crafts/home.html>

Bassett, Mark. *American Art Pottery Wall Pockets*. Atglen, Pennsylvania: Schiffer Publishing, 2004.

_____. *Introducing Roseville Pottery*. Atglen, Pennsylvania: Schiffer Publishing, 1999.

"Big Gain Reported in N.Y. Pottery and Glass Sales." *Ceramic Industry*, January 1935.

Brighton, Stephen A. "Prices that Suit the Times: Shopping for Ceramics at The Five Points." *Society for Historical Archaeology* 35(3), 2001.

"Buying Continues Active at Los Angeles, Chicago." *Ceramic Industry*, March 1942.

Curator of Ceramics. Smithsonian National Museum of American History, Behring Center. Personal communication, March 16, 2004.

Davis, Vivan. "Highlights on Pottery." *Better Homes & Gardens*, October 1936.

Deetz, James J. F. "Ceramics From Plymouth, 1620-1835: The Archaeological Evidence." In Quimby, Ian M.G. (ed.) *Ceramics in America*. Charlottesville, Virginia: The University Press of Virginia, 1973.

Devlin, Peter. "The Passion of Collecting." *The Lantern*, 1999 <http://staffweb. library.northwestern.edu/ thelantern/sept1999/collecting.html>

Druesedow, Jean L., Curator. "Uncommon Clay: Ohio Art Pottery from the Paige Palmer Collection." Kent State University. Broadbent Gallery. October 25, 2000 to October 28, 2001.

"F. H. Rhead Returns from European Tour." *Ceramic Industry*, September 1937.

Fontana, Bernard L. "The Cultural Dimensions of Pottery: Ceramics as Social Documents." In Quimby, Ian M.G. (ed.) *Ceramics in America*. Charlottesville, Virginia: The University Press of Virginia, 1973.

Gibney, Raymond G. "Best Business in Years '42 Pittsburgh Show." *Ceramic Industry*, February 1942.

"Giftware Sales Up 55%." *Ceramics Industry*, September 1941.

Gilchrist, Brenda (ed.). *The Smithsonian Illustrated Library of Antiques. Pottery*. Washington, D.C.: Smithsonian Institution, 1981.

Grant, Tracey. "Weller Woodcraft and Forest." *WPA Press* XII, March 2002.

"Hardware Stores and Ceramic Gift Lines." *Ceramic Industry*, October 1942.

Hay, Jane. *Christie's Collectibles. Art Deco Ceramics. The Connoisseur's Guide*. Boston, Massachusetts: Little, Brown and Company, 1996.

Henzke, Lucile. *Art Pottery of America*. Revised 3rd Edition. Atglen, Pennsylvania: Schiffer Publishing, 1999.

Hume, Ivor Noël. *If These Pots Could Talk*. Milwaukee, Wisconsin: Chipstone Foundation, 2001.

Husfloen, Klye and Pat McPherson (eds.). *Antique Trader® Pottery & Porcelain Ceramics Price Guide*. 4th Edition. Iola, Wisconsin: Krause Publications, 2003.

Huxford, Sharon and Bob. *The Collectors Encyclopedia of Weller Pottery*. Paducah, Kentucky: Collector Books, 1979.

Jackman, Bob. "Monumental Weller Vase Fetches $112,500." *Maine Antique Digest*, 1997.

Johnson, Don. "Rookwood VII and Keramics 1997." *Maine Antique Digest*, September 1997.

_____. "Rookwood XII, Art Pottery and Art Glass Auction." *Maine Antique Digest*, September 2002.

Kaeppel, H. V. "The Roving Reporter on the West Coast." *Ceramic Industry*, February 1938.

Kamerling, Bruce. "Anna and Albert Valentien: The Arts and Crafts Movement in San Diego." *The Journal of San Diego History* 24 (3) Summer 1978.

Kenefick, Kari. "Weller Pottery 1872-1948." *WPA Press*, Vol. 8, April 2001.

Kerr, Ann. *Collector's Encyclopedia of Russel Wright*. Paducah, Kentucky: Collector Books, 1998.

Kientz, Rene. "Harried potters: Roseville made magic for decades." *Houston Chronicle*, November 29, 2002.

Korzendorfer, Lois (compiler). "Decorative Objects: Guides to Hallmarks, Marks, Markers and Companies. A Selected List of References." *Main Reading Room*, Library of Congress, 1988. <http://www.loc.gov/rr/main/gopher/decorat.html>

Kovel, Ralph and Terry. *Kovels' American Art Pottery.* New York: Crown Publishers, Inc., 1993.

Levin, Elaine. *The History of American Ceramics, 1607 to the Present. From Pipkins and Bean Pots to Contemporary Forms.* New York: Harry N. Abrams, Inc., 1988.

Lilienfeld, Bonnie. "An Honor As Well As A Business Advantage American Art Potters And The Smithsonian, 1885-1913." *Style: 1900's*, Spring 2001.

Lukens, Glen. "American Ceramics – Worth Fighting About, and For." *Ceramic Industry.* August 1945.

"Making the Rounds of the Markets. Reports from the Summer Gift and Art Shows." *Ceramic Industry*, September 1940.

Mason Color & Chemical Works, Inc. "Ceramic Colors: History, Development, Usage." *Ceramic Industry*, November 1979.

McCollam, Anne. "Umbrella stand pops up in value." *Copley News Service*, November 11, 2003.

McDonald, Ann Gilbert. *All About Weller: A History and Collector's Guide to Weller Pottery, Zanesville, Ohio.* Marietta, Ohio: Antique Publications, 1989.

_____. "The Working Women of Weller. The Story of Two Weller Artists During the Great Depression." *Antiques & Collecting Magazine*, October 1997 No. 102 (8).

"Movements in Twentieth-century Art Before World War II." <http://daphne. palomar.edu/mhudelson/StudyGuides/20thCentEarly_WA.html>

Newcomb, Rexford, Jr. "The Ceramic Industry, Now and Postwar." *Bulletin of the American Ceramic Society* 24(2), 1945.

"The Noble Craftsmen We Promote: The Arts and Crafts Movement in the American Midwest. Arts and Crafts in the Decorative Arts." An Exhibit at the Ward M. Canaday Center for Special Collections, Carlson Library, The University of Toledo. March 26th-June 30th, 1999.

Piña, Leslie. *Pottery. Modern Wares. 1920-1960.* Atglen, Pennsylvania: Schiffer Publishing, 1994.

Pratt, Michael. *Mid-Century Modern Dinnerware: Ak-Sar-Ben to Pope-Gosser.* Atglen, Pennsylvania: Schiffer Publishing, 2003.

Quimby, Ian M.G. (ed.) *Ceramics in America.* Charlottesville, Virginia: The University Press of Virginia, 1973.

Rhead, Frederick Hürten. "More About Color." *Crockery and Glass Journal*, vol. 120, 1937.

Ryan, David. "Art Nouveau in Europe." <http://www.artsmia.org/ Modernism/e_ANE.html>

Schneider, Mike. *The Complete Cookie Jar Book.* 4th Edition. Atglen, Pennsylvania: Schiffer Publishing, 2003.

"Skull humidor appraised by Riley Humler of Cincinnati Art Galleries in Cincinnati, Ohio." "Antiques Road Show." January 10, 2000. <http://www.pbs.org/ wgbh/pages/roadshow/series/highlights/2000/Columbus.html>

Snyder, Jeffrey B. "American Artwares of the Depression Era." *Unravel the Gavel*, n.d.

_____. *Depression Pottery.* Atglen, Pennsylvania: Schiffer Publishing, 1999.

_____. *Fiesta: Homer Laughlin China Company's Colorful Dinnerware.* 3rd Edition. Atglen, Pennsylvania: Schiffer Publishing, 2000.

_____. *Hall China.* Atglen, Pennsylvania: Schiffer Publishing, 2002.

Snyder, Jeffrey B. and Leslie Bockol. *Majolica. British, American, & European Wares.* 2nd Edition. Atglen, Pennsylvania: Schiffer Publishing, 2001.

Toy, Jo. "Collecting pottery." *Stoke-on-Trent City Council Libraries*, 2000.

_____. "Frederick Hürten Rhead: a short biography of the pottery designer." *Stoke-on-Trent City Council Libraries.* Hanley, England: Stoke-on-Trent City Council, 2000.

"Two Structural Clay Products Firms Make Success at Pottery." *Ceramic Industry*, May 1935.

"Uses Pottery In Promotion Scheme." *Ceramic Industry*, June 1937.

Ward, Betty and Nancy Schiffer. *Weller, Roseville, and related Zanesville Art Pottery and Tiles.* Atglen, Pennsylvania: Schiffer Publishing, 2000.

"Weller Pottery 1872-1948 Fultonham & Zanesville Ohio." Wisconsin Pottery Association. 2002, pp. 1-4. <http://wisconsinpottery.org/Weller/weller2001show/ weller2001exhibit.html>

"Weller Timeline." <http://Wisconsinpottery.org/Weller/timeline.html>

Appendix

Weller Line Names

What follows is a listing of the known lines produced by this long-lived and prolific firm. As time goes by and research continues, this list will no doubt expand. Line names in italics indicate that the line is illustrated in the text.

Alvin
Ansonia
Arcadia
Arcola
Ardsley
Art Nouveau: a.k.a. L'Art Nouveau
Atlantic
Atlas
Aurelian
Auroro: a.k.a. Aurora, Auroral
Baldin
Barcelona
Bedford Green Matt
Besline
Blo'Red
Blossom
Blue Drapery
Blue Ware
Bo Marblo
Bonito
Bouquet
Breton
Brighton
Bronze Ware
Burnt Wood
Cactus
Cameo Jewel: a.k.a. Cameo Jewell, Jewell
Chase
Chelsea
Chengtu
Clarmont
Classic
Claywood
Cloudburst
Colored Glaze
Comet
Coppertone
Copra
Cornish

Creamware
Cretone
Crystalline
Darsie
Delsa
Delta
Dickens Ware I (First Line)
Dickens Ware II (Second Line)
Dickens Ware III (Third Line)
Dorland
Dresden
Dupont
Eclair
Elberta
Eldora
Eocean
Etched Floral
Etched Matt
Ethel
Etna
Euclid
Evergreen
Fairfield
Flemish
Fleron
Floral
Florala
Florenzo
Floretta
Forest
Fra Bel Ita
Frosted Matt
Fruitone
Fru-Russett
Fudzi
Garden Ware
Geode
Glendale
Gloria
Golbogreen
Golden Glow
Graystone

Greenaways
Greenbriar
Greora
Hobart
Hudson
Hunter
Ivoris
Ivory: a.k.a. Clinton Ivory
Jap Birdimal: a.k.a. Rhead Faience
Jet Black
Juneau
Kenova
Klyro Ware
Knifewood
Lamar: a.k.a. Lemar
LaSa
Lavonia
Lido
Lonhuda
Lorbeek
Loru
Louella
Louwelsa
Lustre: a.k.a. Luster
Majolica
Malta
Malvern
Manhattan
Marengo
Marvo
Matt Green
Matt Ware: a.k.a. Modeled Matt
Melrose
Mi-Flo: a.k.a. MiFlo
Mirror Black
Monochrome
Morocco
Muskota
Narona
Neiska
Nile
Norwood
Noval
Novelties
Novelty Line
Oak Leaf
Oriental
Orris
Panella

Paragon
Parian
Pastel
Patra
Patricia
Pearl
Perfecto
Pictorial
Pierre
Pinecone
Pumila
Racene
Ragenda
Raydence
Roba
Rochelle
Roma
Rosemont
Rubina
Rudlor
Sabrinian
Selma
Seneca
Senic
Sicard: a.k.a. Sicardo
Silvertone
Softone
Souevo
Stellar
Sydonia
Teakwood
Terose
Tile
Ting
Tivoli
Tupelo
Turada
Turkis
Tutone
Underglaze Blue Ware
Utility Ware
Velva
Velvetone
Voile
Warwick
Wayne Ware
Wild Rose
Woodcraft
Wood Rose: a.k.a. Woodrose
Xenia
Zona

Index

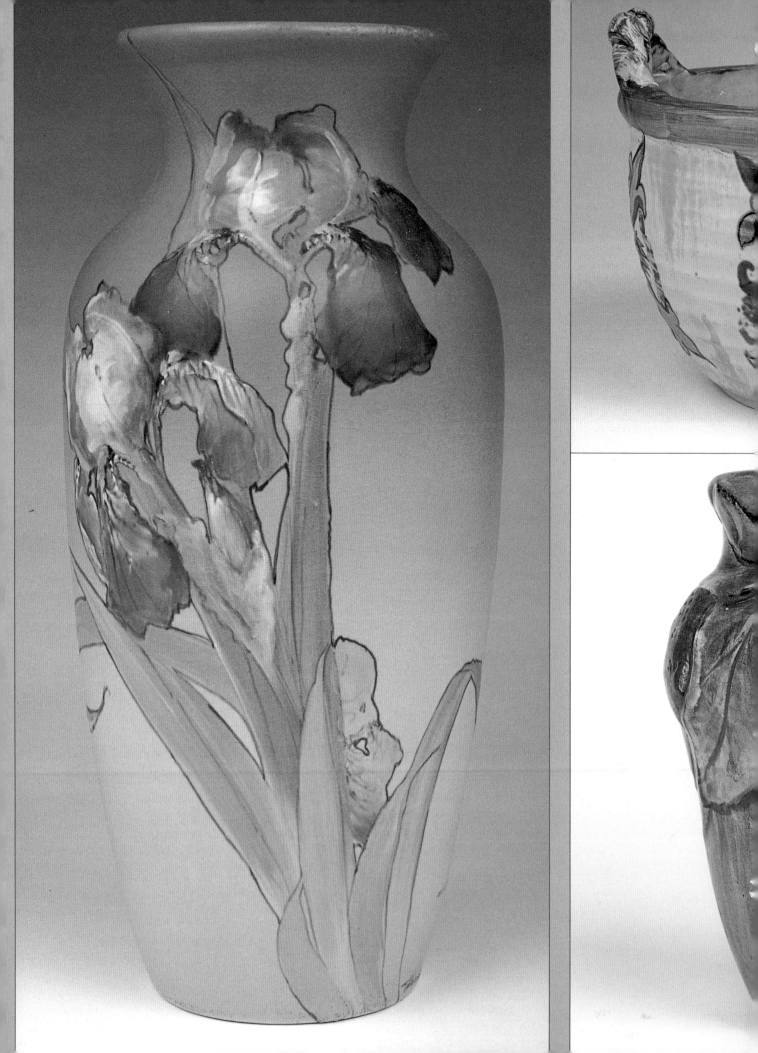